HILARIOUS FISHING CARTOONS

HILARIOUS FISHING CARTOONS

John Troy
Color by Doris Troy

With a Foreword by Nick Lyons

Skyhorse Publishing

Skyhorse Publishing books may be purchased in bulk at special discounts for sales promotion, corporate gifts, fund raising, or educational purposes. Special editions can also be created to specifications. For details, contact Special Sales Department, Skyhorse Publishing, 555 Eighth Avenue, Suite 903, New York, NY 10018 or info@skyhorsepublishing.com.

www.skyhorsepublishing.com

Library of Congress Cataloging-in-Publication Data
    Troy, John.
    Hilarious fishing cartoons / John Troy ; color by Doris Troy ; with a foreword by Nick Lyons.
        p.   cm.
    ISBN-13: 978-1-60239-304-2
    1. Fishing in art.   2. American wit and humor, Pictorial.   I. Title.

    NC1429.T695A4   2007
    741.5'6973—dc22

                                                                    2007020064

10   9   8   7   6   5   4   3   2   1

Printed in China

To Doris,
my wife, my life

FOREWORD

"I've never gone fishing," a serious friend once told me, "when I haven't caught myself laughing half a dozen times, even when I'm alone." That's my experience, too. The thousand facets of the sport and those who practice it seem ideally suited to humor—though really good humor in any field is rare.

I once told a group of fishermen the true story of a fellow who got a fly caught in his lips when a brisk upstream gust of wind whisked the fly back and pinned both lips together. The man could not bear to stop fishing and went the entire day, mumbling, with the fly in his lips. Later, his face swelled mightily and he almost died. A listener said, with solemn authority, "Now that's a *real* fisherman."

Of course, the man was just a lunatic, but many moments on the water, or in the homes of addicted fishermen, border on the tragic but share elements of humor (often black) too. You'll find a dozen brands of humor in this collection of John Troy's delicious cartoons:

The fly fisherman freighted with so much equipment there's barely room to see his gleeful and contented smile.

The prophet heralding "The end is near" to salmon surging upstream.

The mad excitement—and peril—of fishing a storm front, with lightning and twenty-foot waves, as one fisherman tells his terrified partner that one hasn't "lived" until he's fished in such weather.

The boat ready to go over a treacherous waterfall and one fisherman invoking the one hooked to a good fish to "Keep a tight line," which can scarcely save them.

The fisherman on a desert island who has managed to hang up on the one palm tree.

The fisherman standing on the head of a monstrous trout and speculating, "I like to think there's a *lunker* in every pool that I fish."

And my great favorite: the man casting from the prow of a crowded lifeboat in treacherous seas, and one of the ship-wrecked calling out, "For the love of God, man, switch to wets. They'll never rise in seas like this."

The humor is zany, sly, brilliant, and memorable. No humorist—not since the late Ed Zern, in words—has captured the whacky, offbeat, hilarious world of the addicted angler so sharply. These cartoons will help any reader better understand the addicted angler—and no angler will fail to laugh at the many-sided portrait of the breed.

—NICK LYONS

ACKNOWLEDGMENTS

This book of cartoons owes its life to the many publishers, editors, art directors, and art editors who throughout my life bought my cartoons. Their wisdom is measured by each laugh we shared, sometimes thousands of miles apart. I thank you, deeply.

—JOHN TROY

INTRODUCTION

A cartoon is a way of telling a story in one picture. And, generally, in a humorous way. Most cartoons, especially single-panel cartoons, and gag cartoons in particular, are simply metaphors for real life. You see this in political cartoons, in magazine cartoons, and mostly in newspaper cartoons.

Why do people turn to the cartoons first when they settle down to read the paper or magazine? Why? Because it makes them feel good, and I'm tempted to say the author of these 200 cartoons is . . . simple. But I won't.

Fishing, by a large margin, is still the most popular sport, with more participants year in and year out than all the other sports combined!

If you find this statement to be stretching it a bit, remember this is being written by a fisherman. Stretching becomes a way of life when two or more fishermen fraternize. Who caught the biggest fish? Why, this award goes to the fisherman who talks last. It's like the fisherman struggling with a large fish on his line. One of the many onlookers asks him, "How big is that fish you have on, Al?" Al replies, "If I land it, it'll be a good two or three pounds. If it gets off, close to ten or fifteen pounds!" Al, here, is not lying. He is speculating. Fishermen speculate a lot. Politicians lie, used-car salesmen lie, so to set the record straight, fishermen speculate and stretch but they never, ever lie.

One of the funny things is that fish are the only creatures that grow after they kick the bucket. For example, many years ago, I was hunting with Cousin Billy (I don't know whose cousin he was; everyone just called him Cousin Billy) and Uncle John alongside an autumn-low trout stream. Cousin Billy caught two trout in a crystal clear pool with a compact fishing outfit he always carried in his game pocket while hunting. One trout, a brown male, was in beautiful spawning colors and about fifteen inches long. The other trout, also a brown, was about ten inches long. The years drifted by. I began writing an outdoor column and did one about Cousin Billy and his two trout. He called me and thanked me for recalling to him the incident that had happened twenty-five years before. He did correct me about the size of the fish. They had grown. And how! Now, the big trout was so big it could have swallowed the small trout, which now was fifteen inches. In that twenty-five years, the trout had grown immensely. Now, another twenty-five years later, I'll bet that trout is at least eight or ten pounds. They never stop growing. And I have a feeling that if Cousin Billy is still around, he'll be calling me soon.

From the wise old brown trout jumping up to criticize the fly fisherman—"I've been admiring your casting, but your choice of flies leaves a lot to be desired"—to the guy who has dragged his recently caught 200 pound shark, still hooked, to a party and is asked by his wife, "Couldn't you just show them the pictures?"—it's all here in its colorful entirety: from the funny things fishermen do, to the funny things that are done to them. If all goes well, they meet on the common ground of laughter.

May I tell you another joke? No? Okay, then turn the page. Let the fun begin!

—JOHN TROY

HILARIOUS FISHING CARTOONS

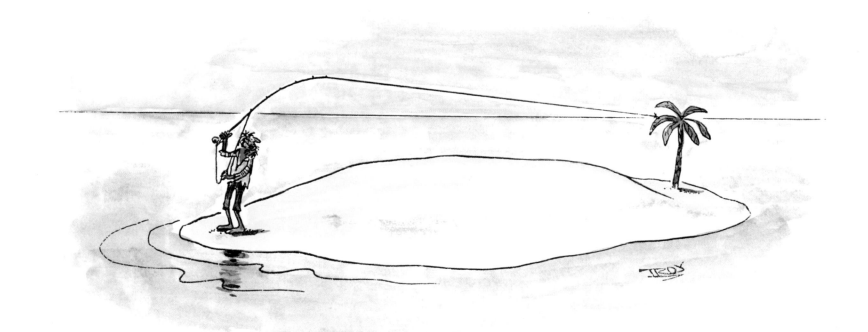

"For the love of God, man, switch to wets . . . They'll never rise in seas like this!"

"This must be the 'worse' part of 'for better or for worse'!"

"It's a good thing our ice fishing gear is in the *trunk*, or our day would really be spoiled!"

"That guy thinks like a fish!"

"You're not going to like this, Pop, but I want to be a fly fisherman."

"I don't get it. I've been casting to that fish for an hour, and it's never moved."

"I love it in the summer when they just wear sneakers and bare legs."

"I can't figure out why I keep getting wind knots."

"Leader shy and angler wise I can put up with—it's his darn insolence that bothers me."

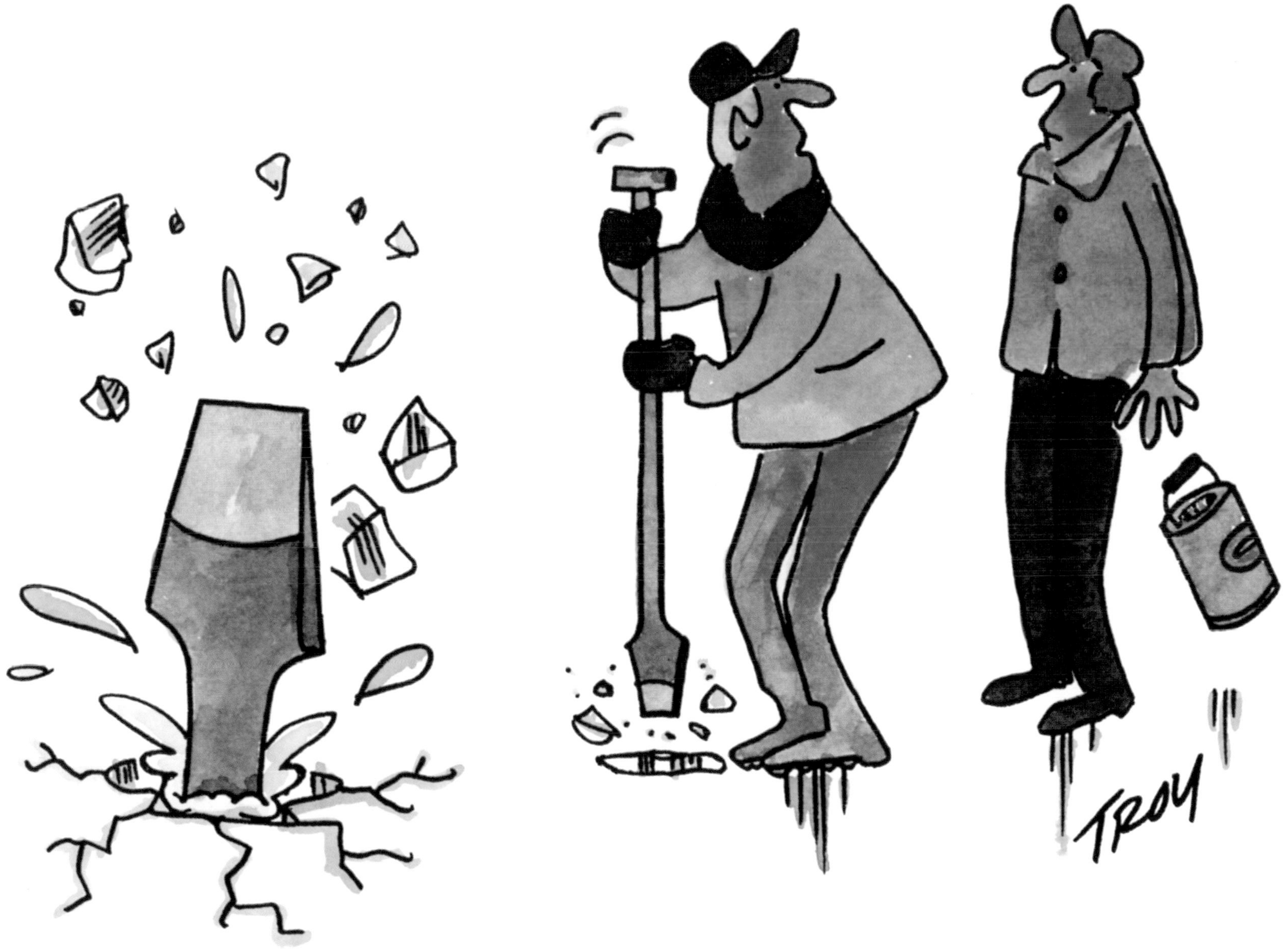
TROY

"Uh-oh."

"Cold front snuck right up on that city feller."

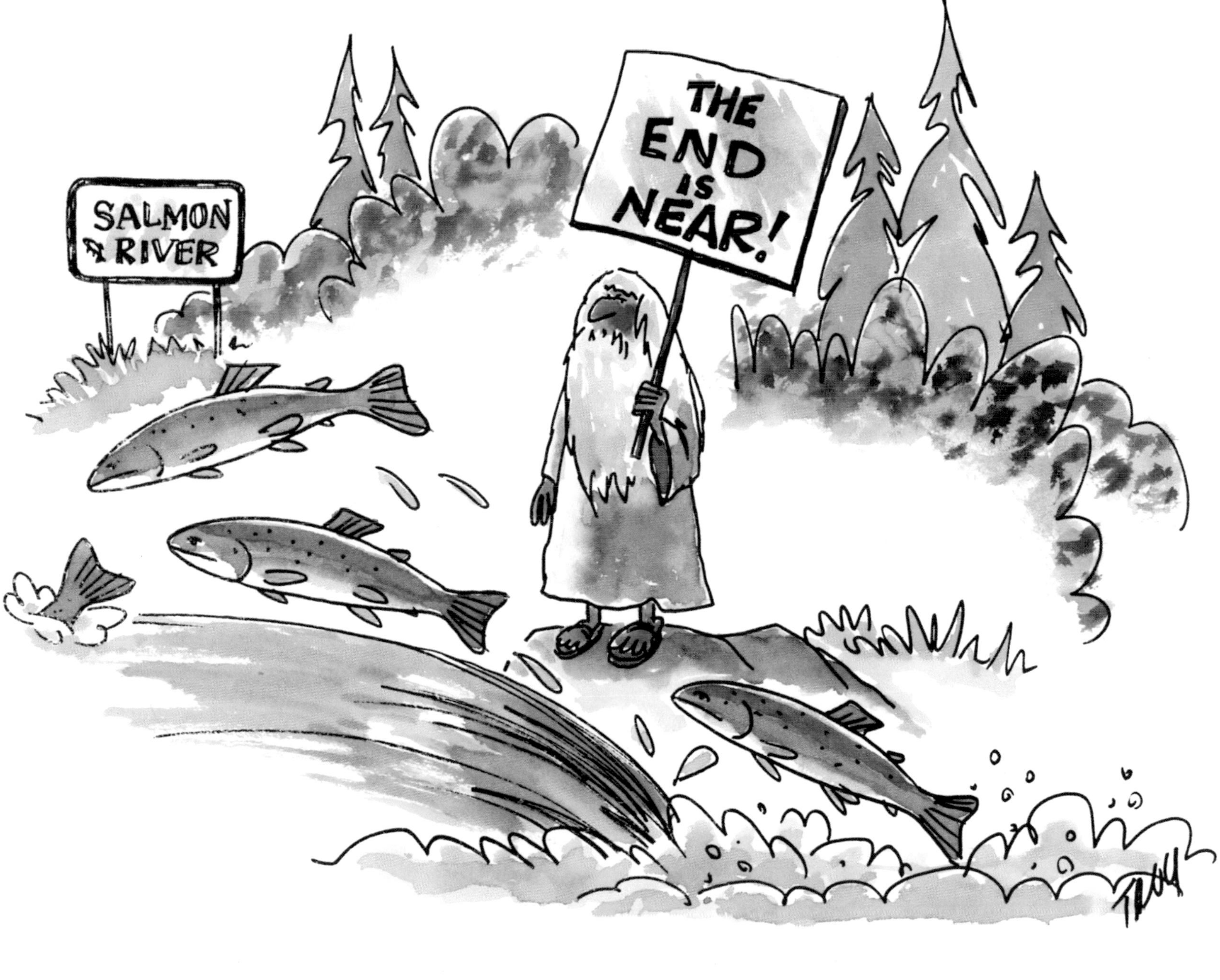
SALMON RIVER
THE END IS NEAR!

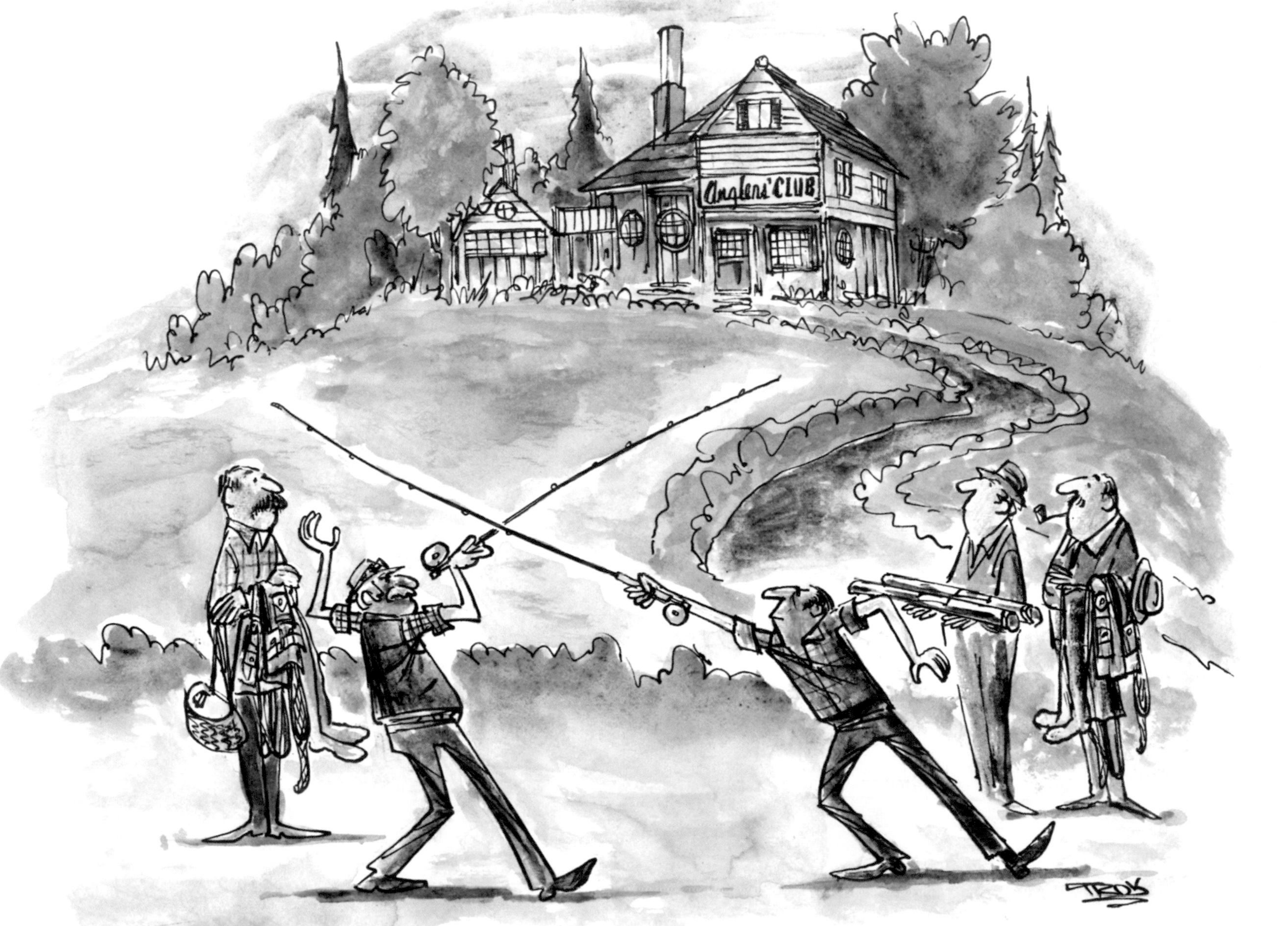
Anglers' CLUB
TROG

"If anybody catches that lunker, it'll probably be Herb."

"No, no, you idiot—it's plastic!"

"Quick! Hit that pocket over there with your Muddler!"

"So, how do you like tube fishing on Lake Michigan?"

"Now here's a little gem the fish just can't resist . . . well, even as I speak!"

"And for added leverage on those extra long casts, here's a handy foot extension."

"Are you kidding? This new custom-made bamboo rod doesn't go near the river!"

"Mr. Bromley is an expert on salmon flies."

"This must be the trophy stretch."

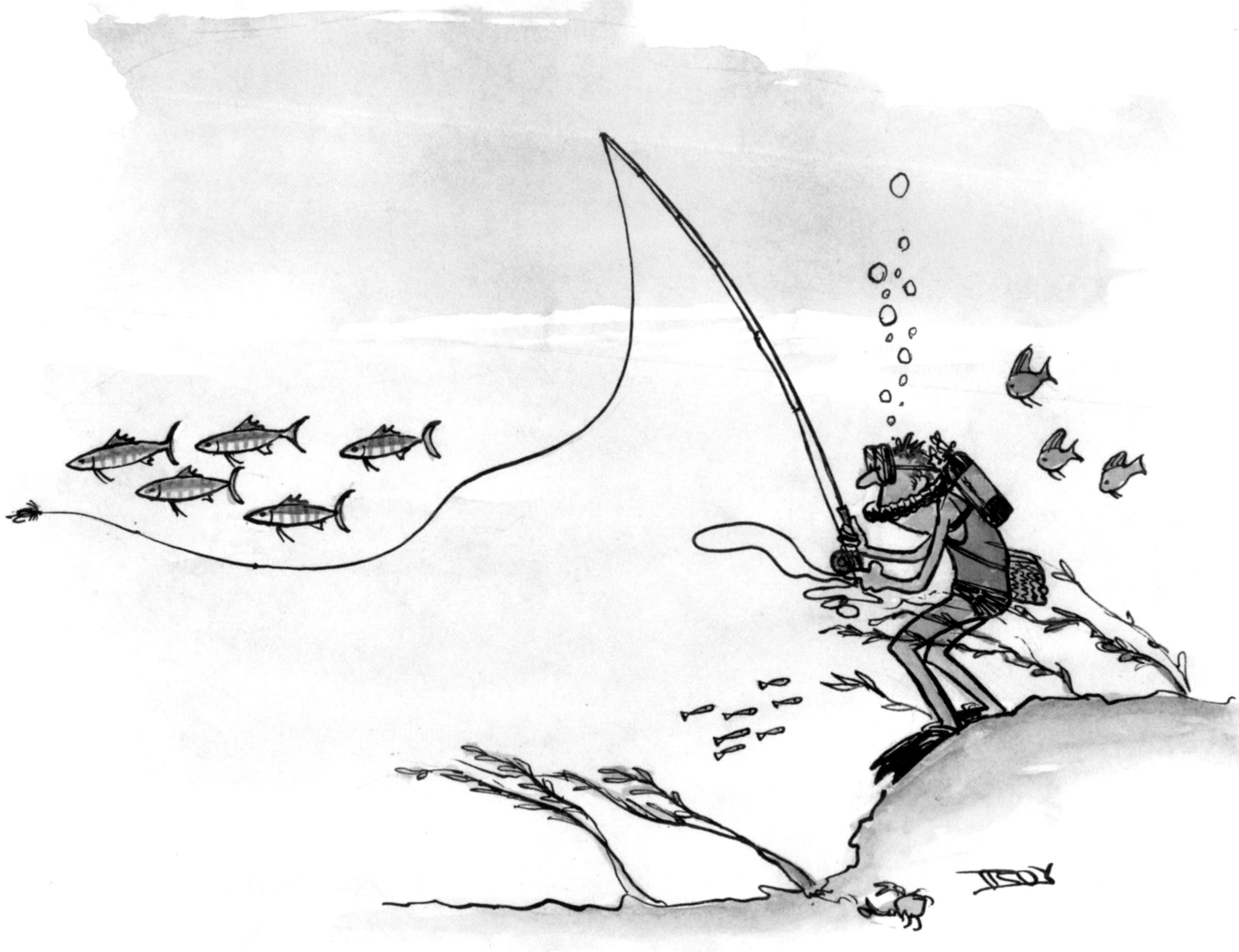

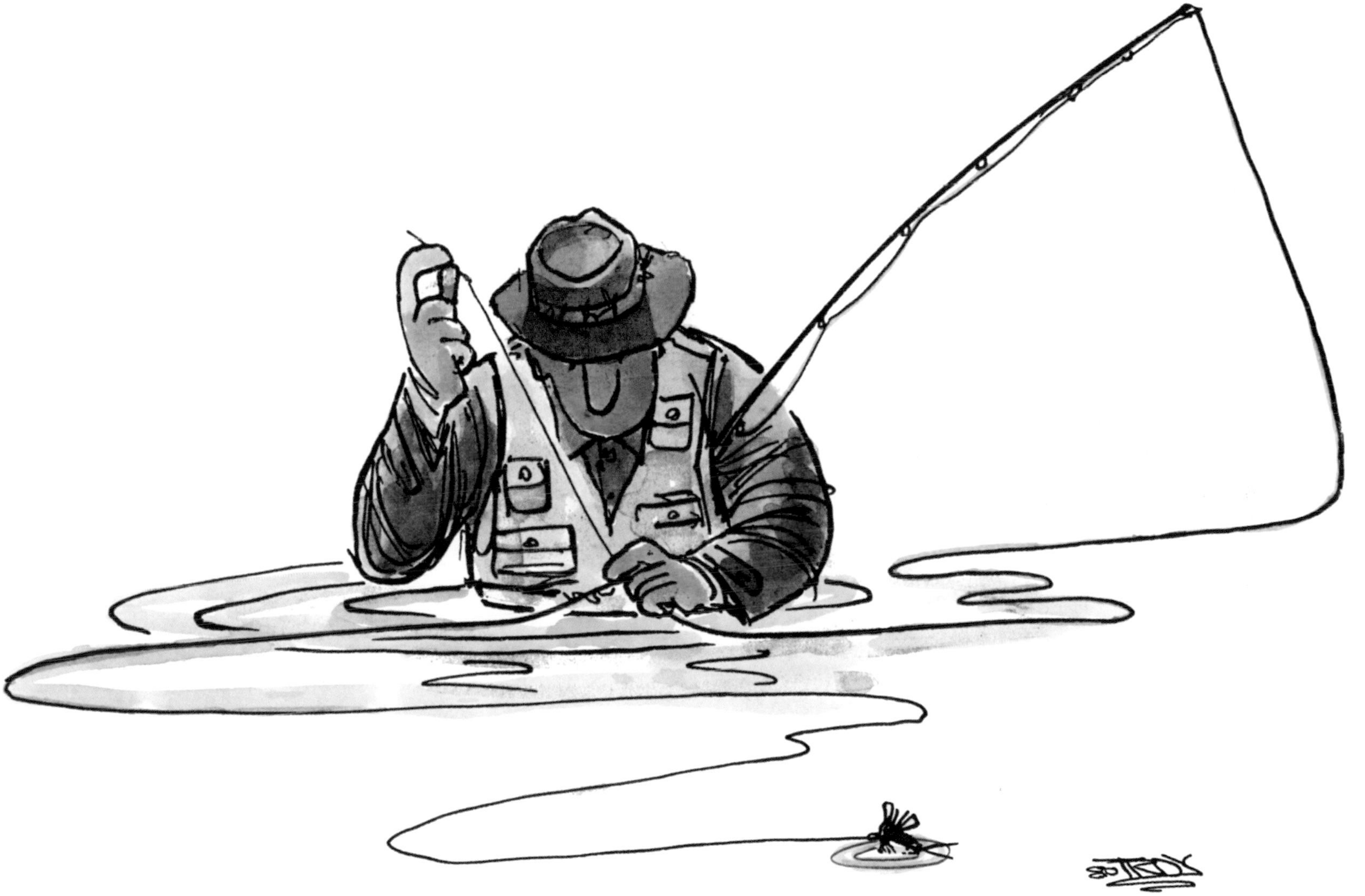

MENDING A CAST

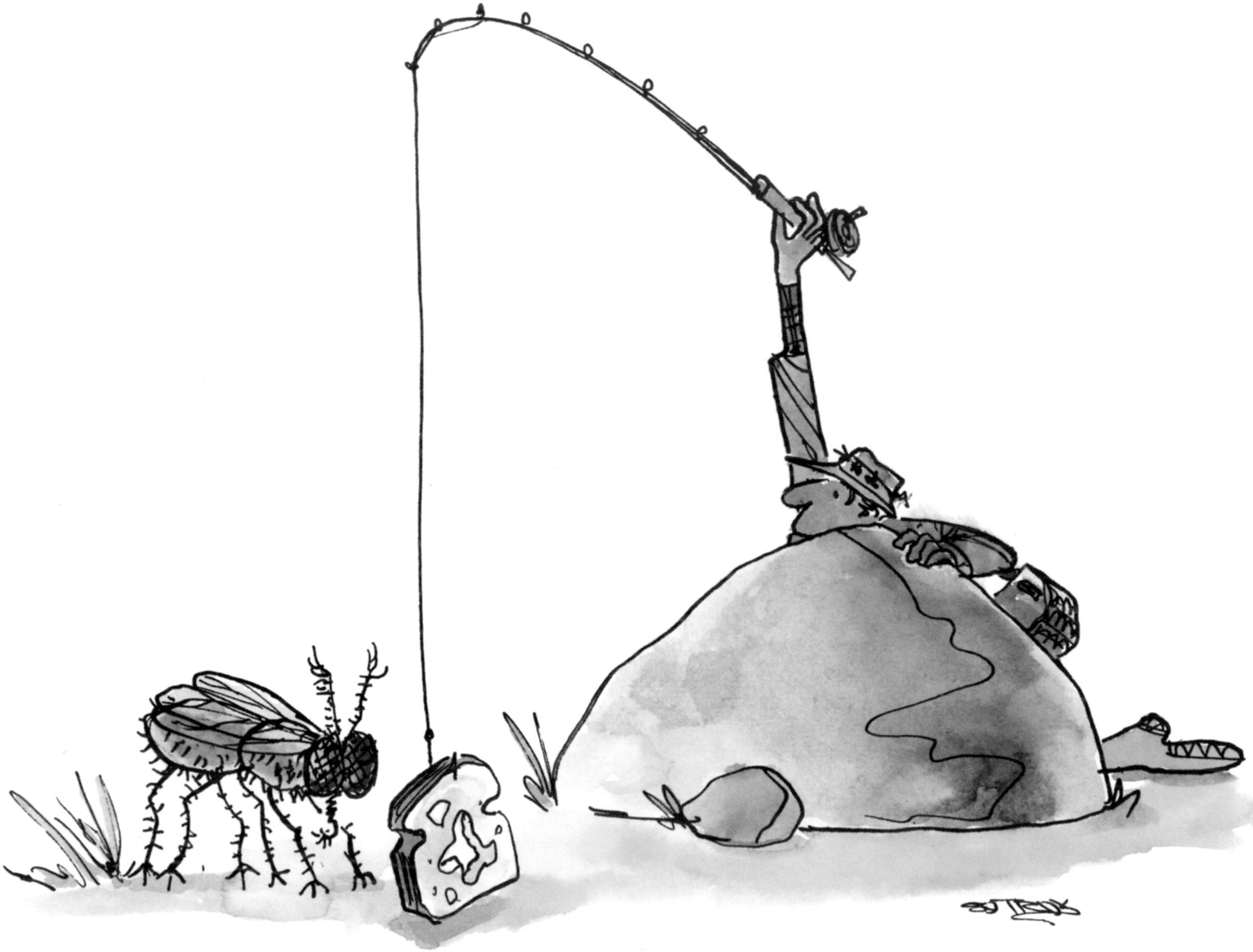

FLY FISHING

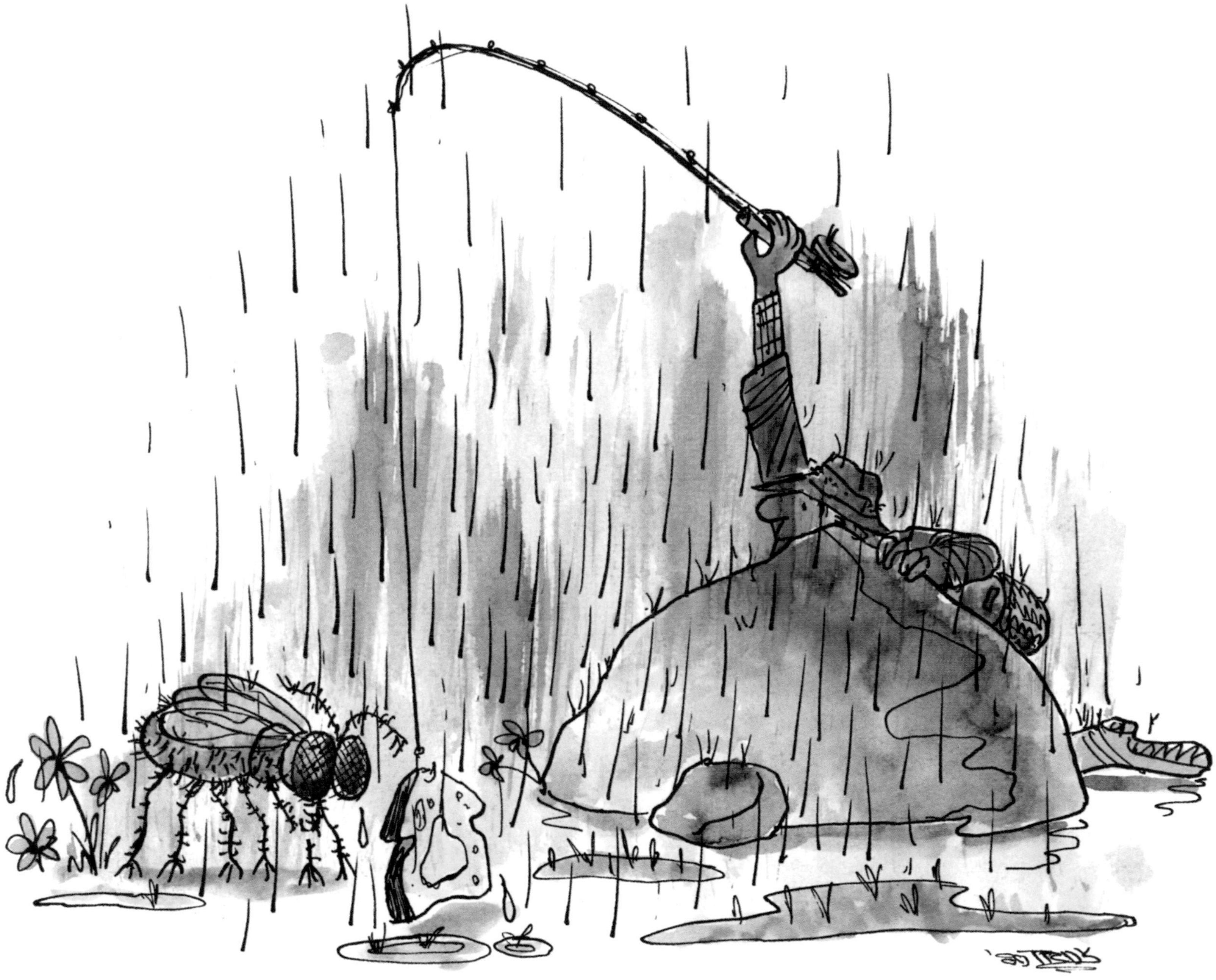

WET FLY FISHING

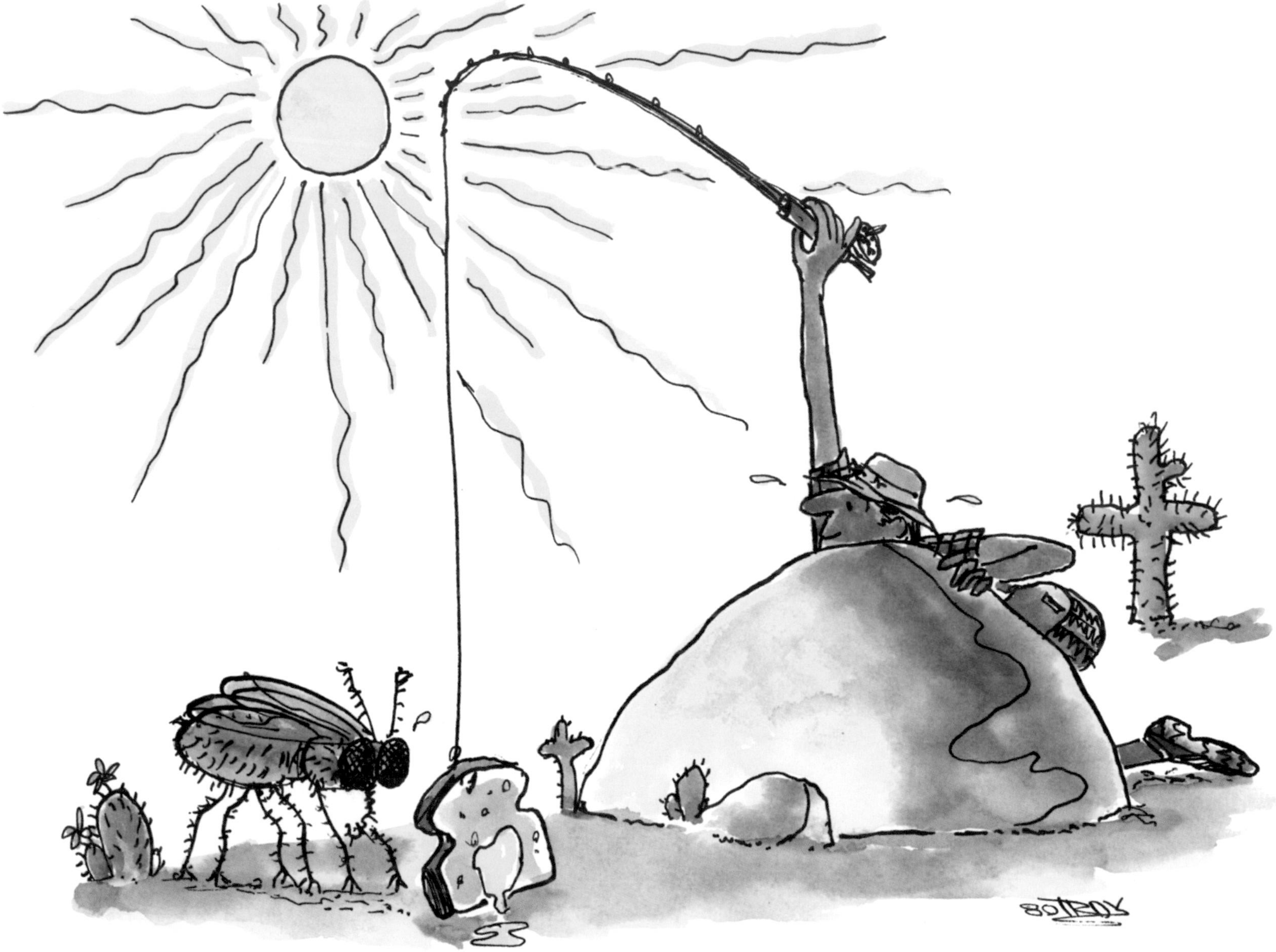

DRY FLY FISHING

"You don't see many rises like this!"

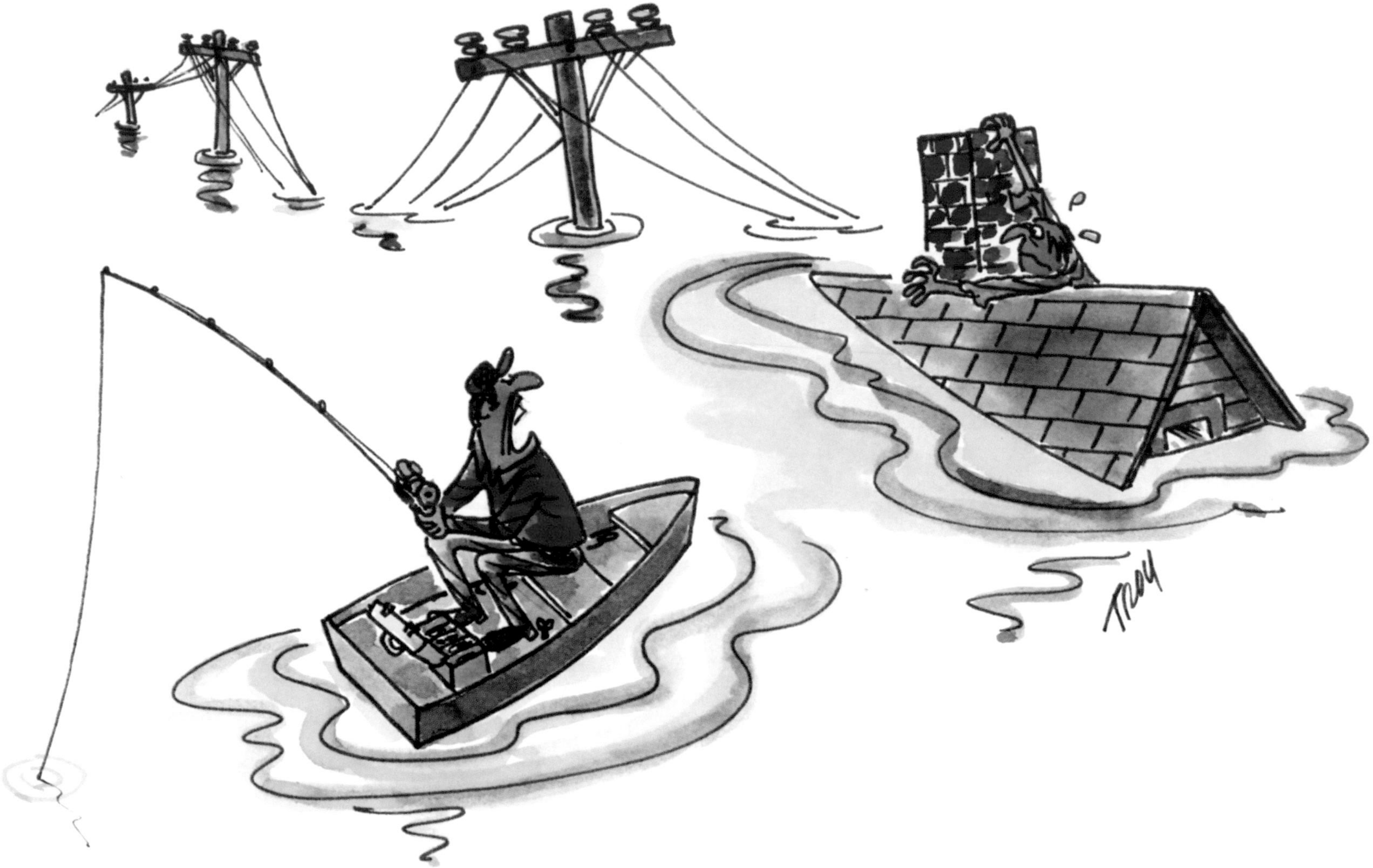
TROY

"You're scaring the fish!"

"Hey Dad, tell me again about the old days and how this stream used to teem with trout."

"I'd feel a lot better about catching that 40-pound muskie if it hadn't eaten my 14-pound bass."

"I felt I was getting too serious about fly-fishing."

"Uh-oh, looks like Al fell off the wagon again."

"Trolling's out of the question. I can't do less than fifty-four miles an hour."

"These walleyes are really deep—I must have ninety feet of line out!"

"Just what I always wanted, Son—a Magforce 12-foot Powercasting Surfbuster."

"I don't go for that sissy tackle!"

"I think we're too early."

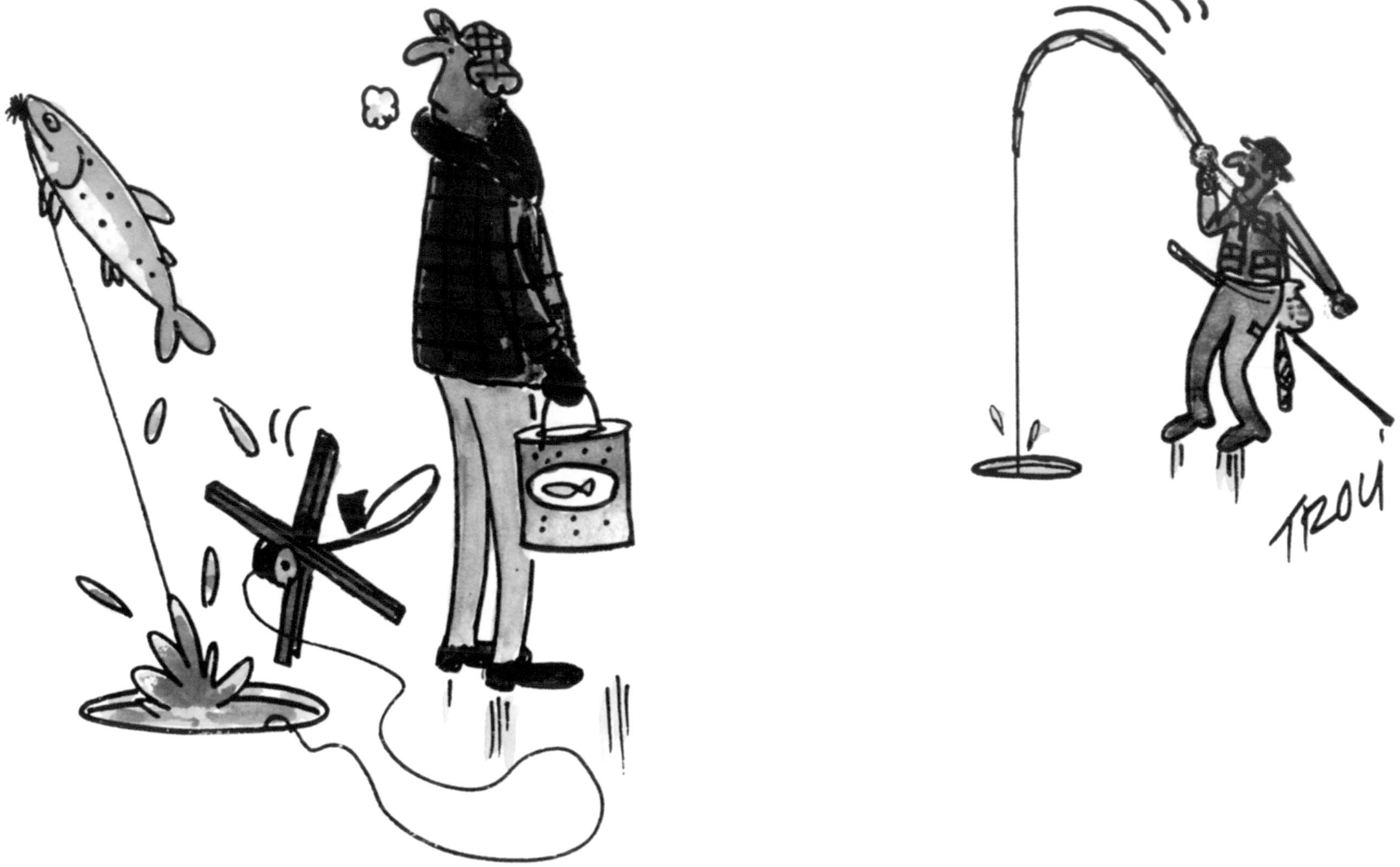
TROU

"I've got one!"

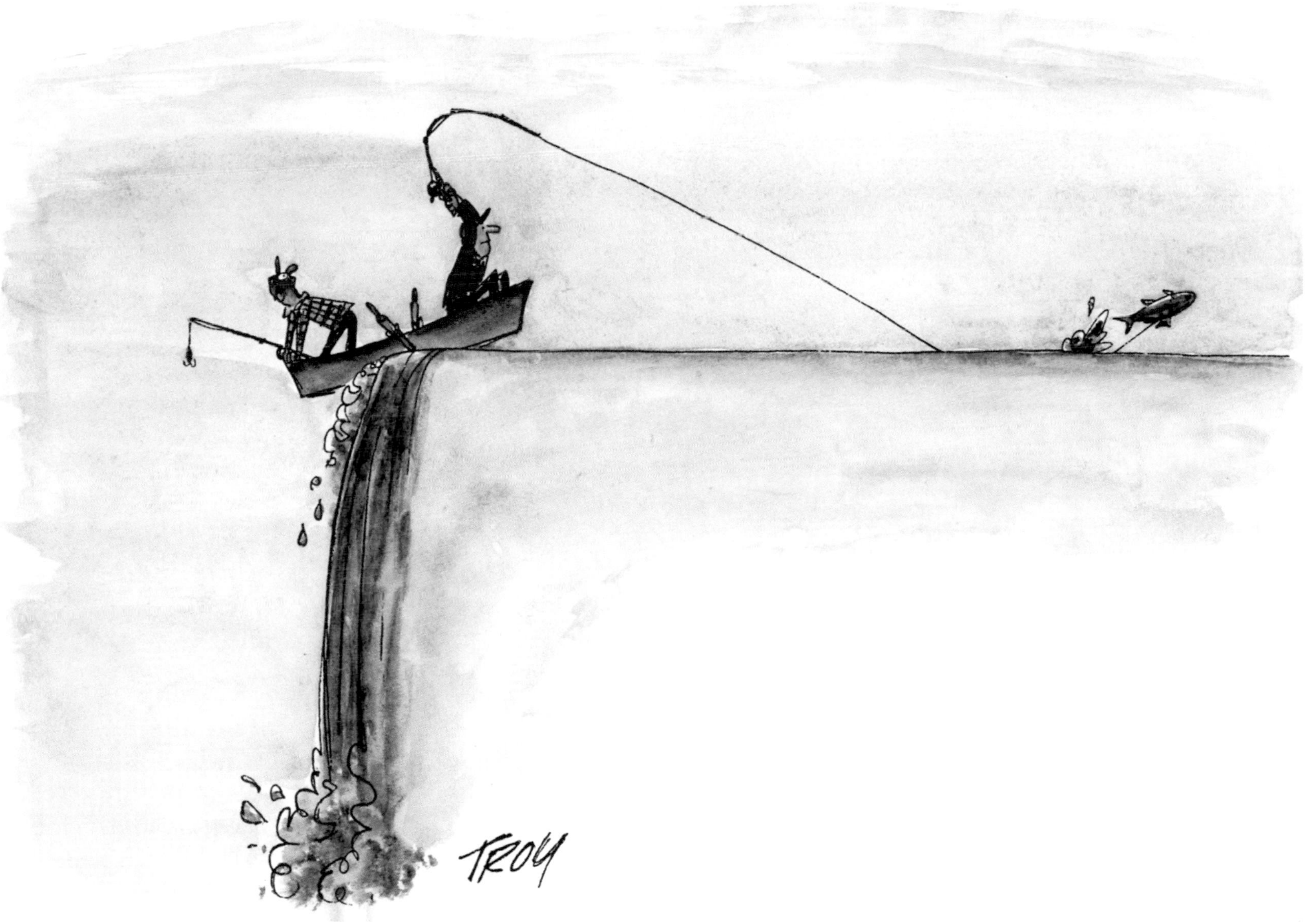
TROY

"Keep a tight line!!!"

"Look at that fishing tackle!"

"You don't see many salmon runs like this one."

Now *that's* what I call a feeding frenzy!"

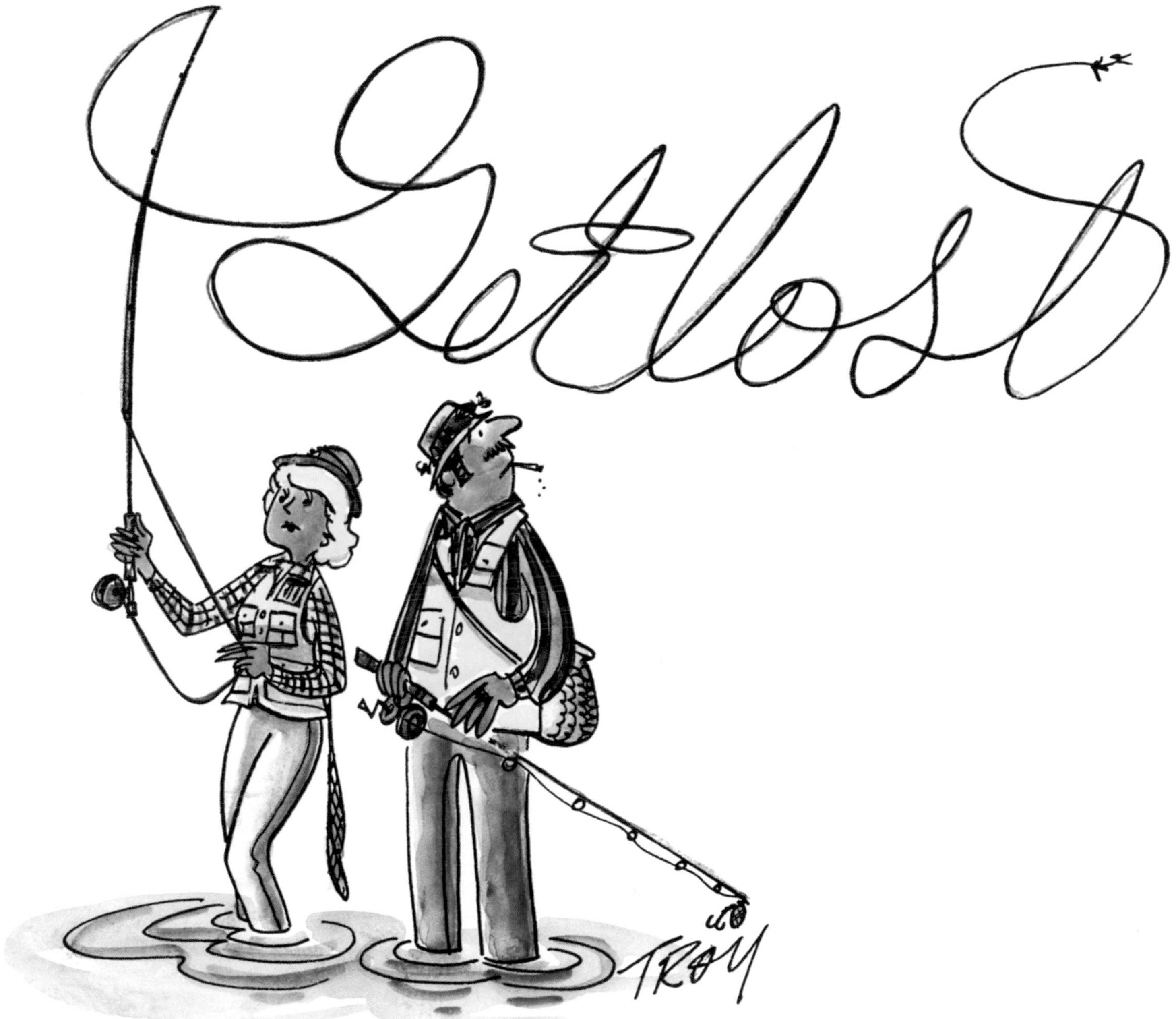

Get lost
TROY

"Edgar hooked a thirty-pound king salmon on his Ultralight. He goes for counseling tomorrow."

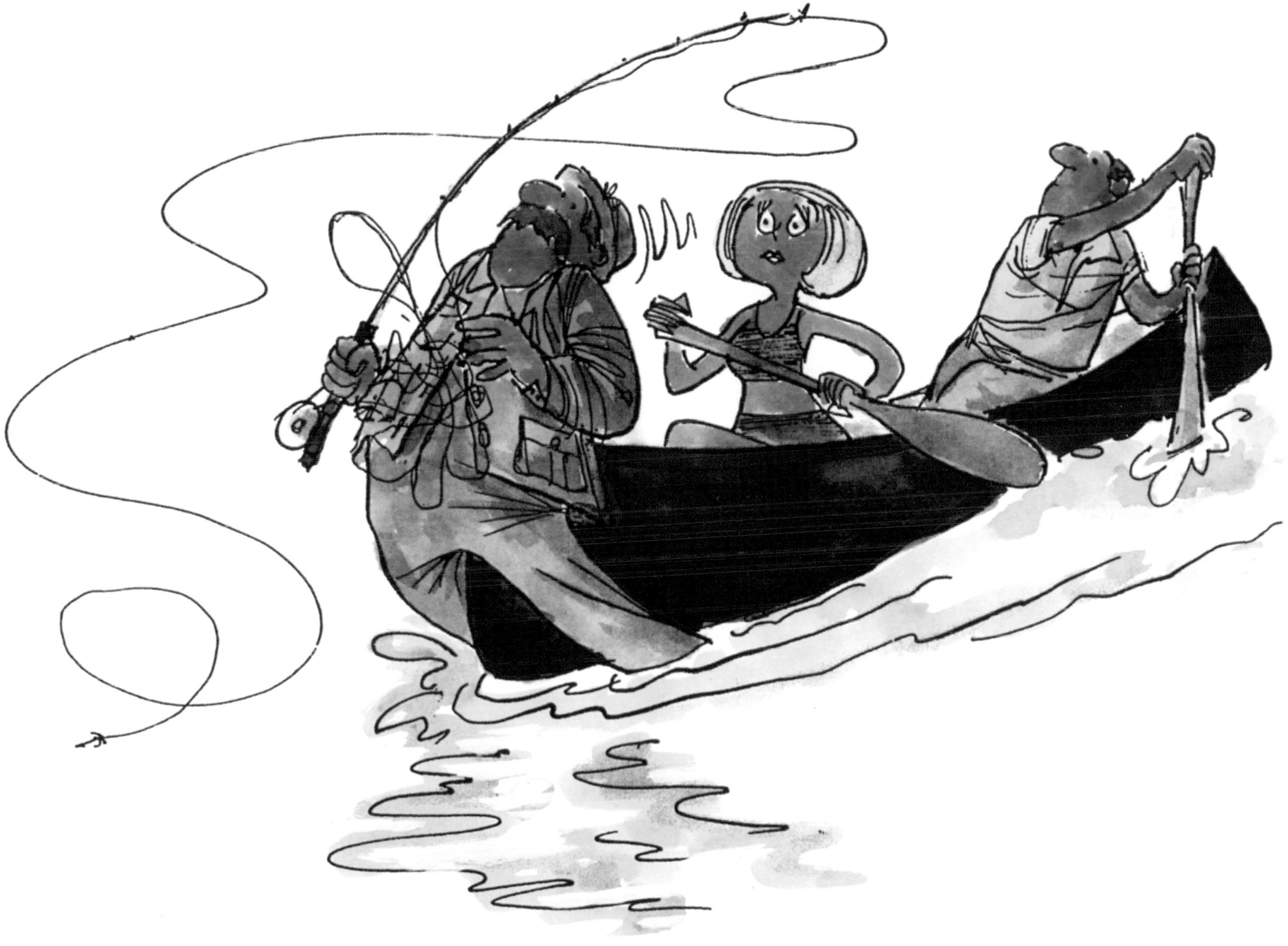

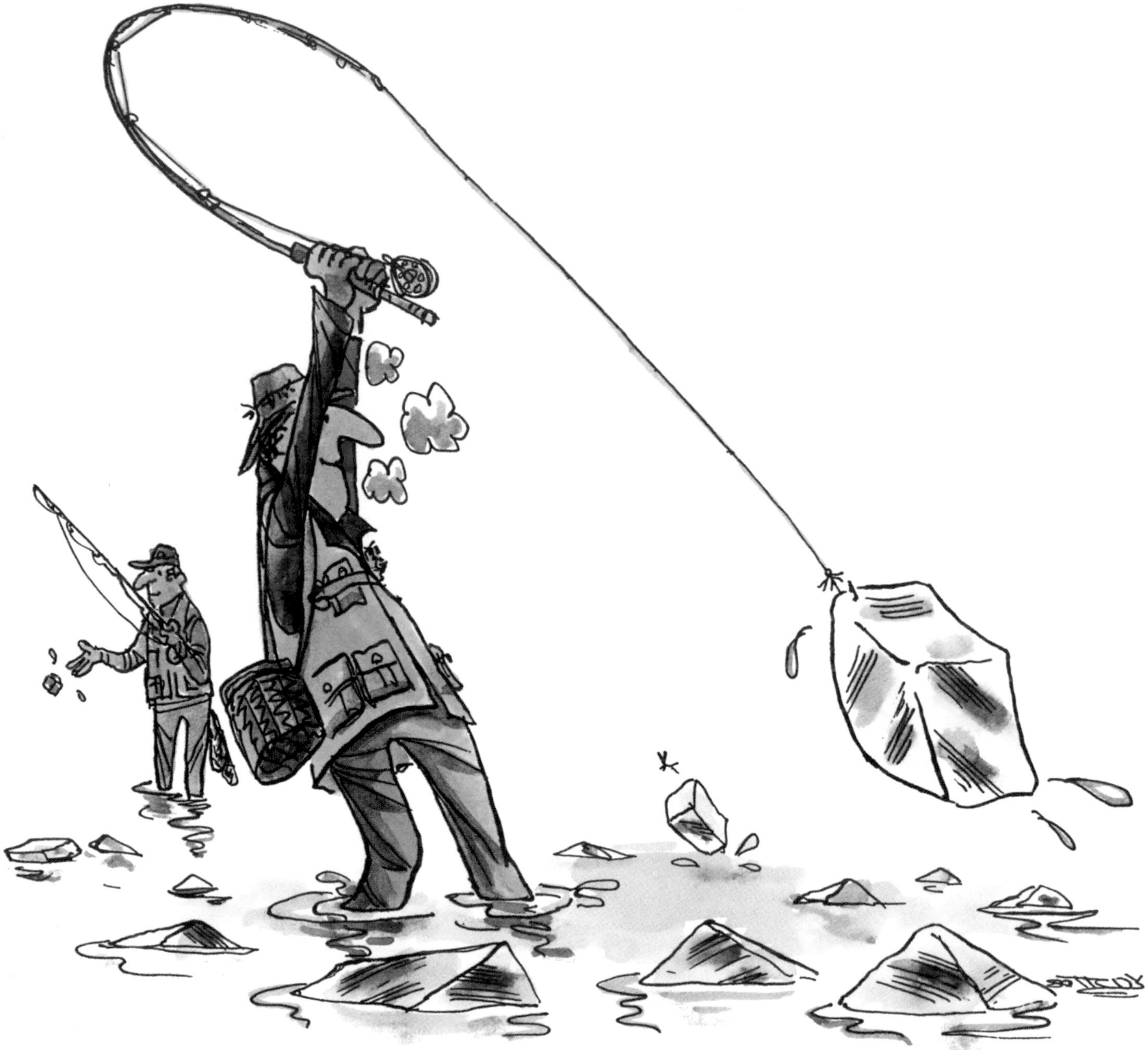

ICE FISHING

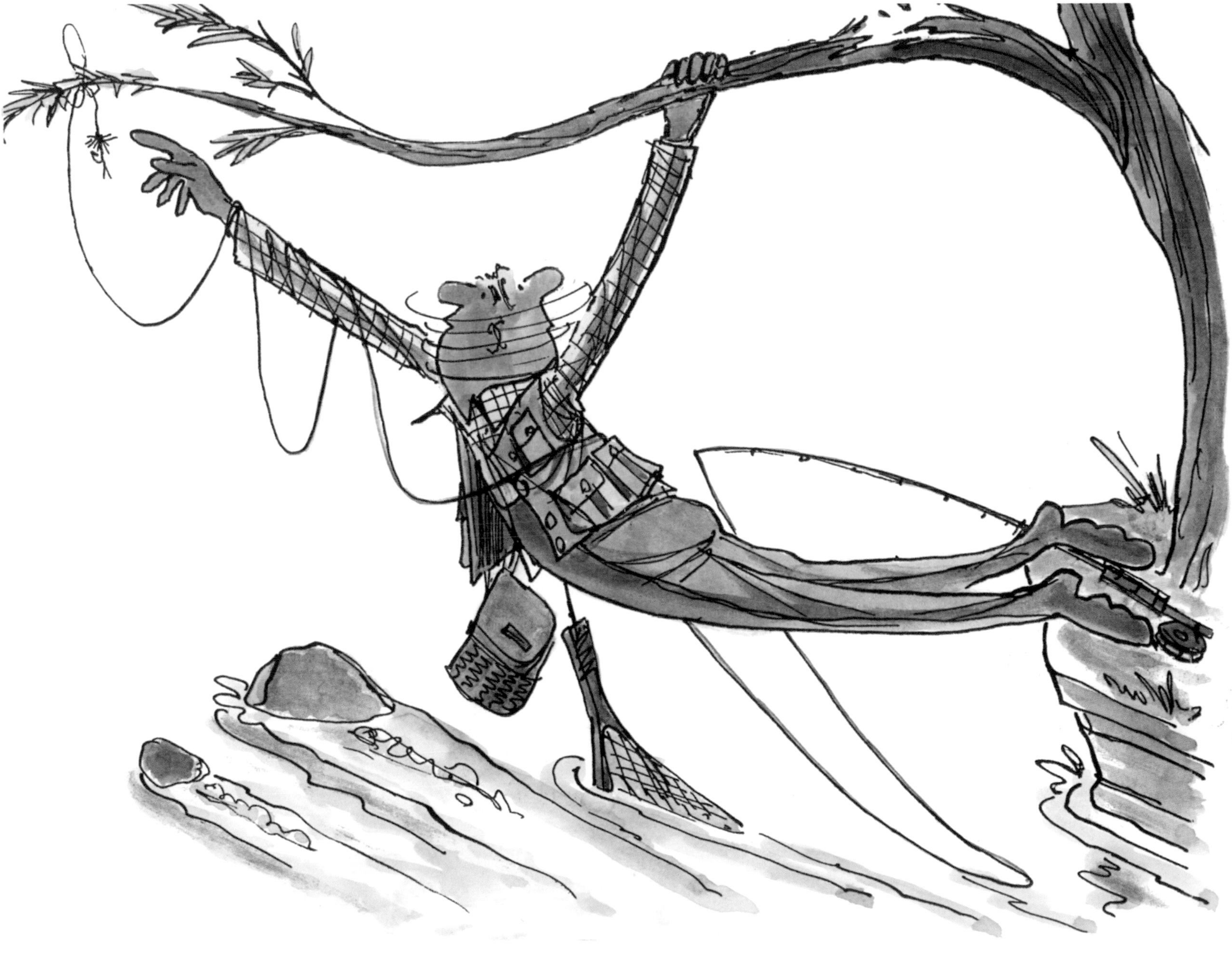

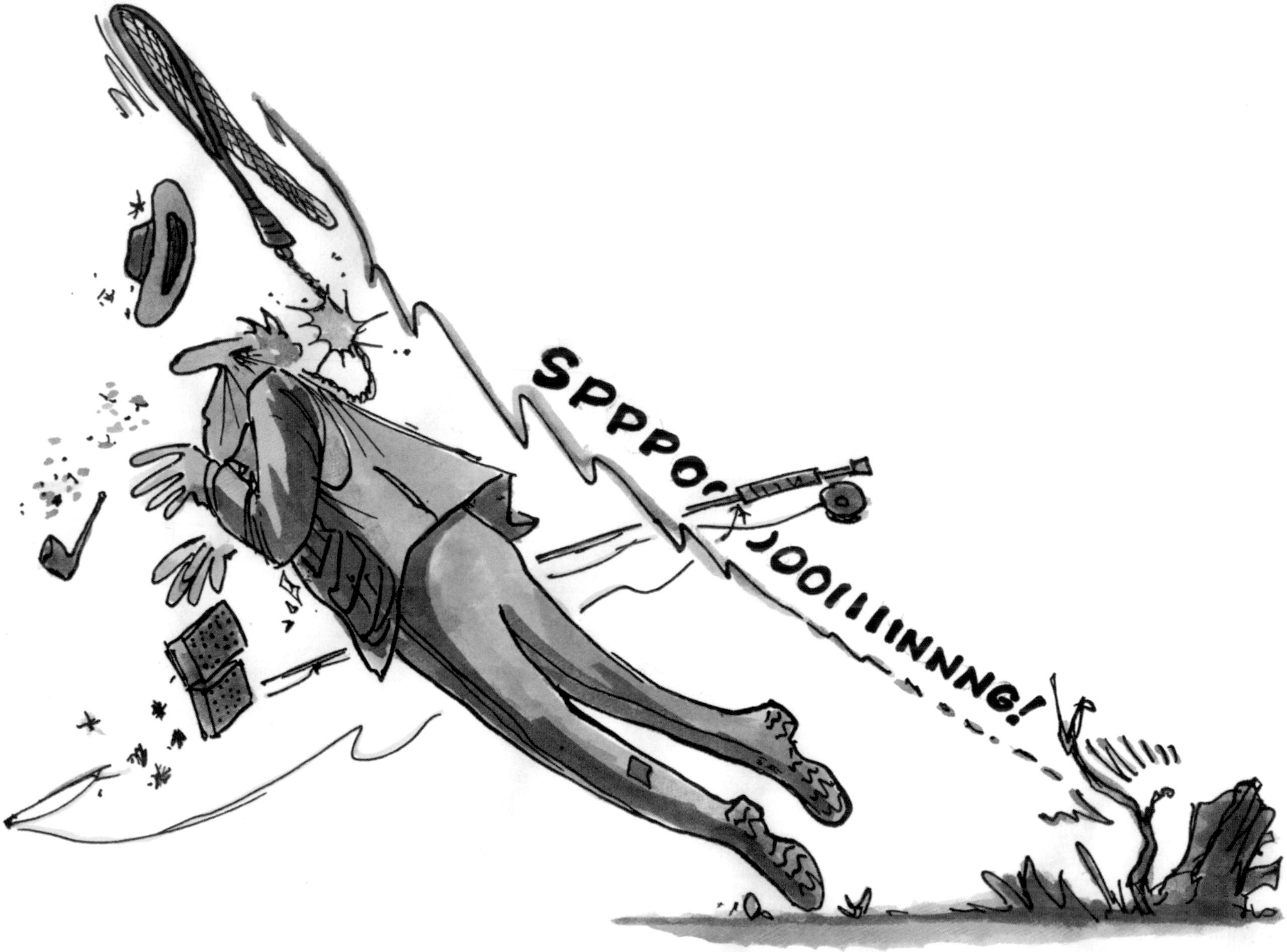
SPPPOOOOOIIIIINNNNG!

TAKING A "SPRING" BREAK

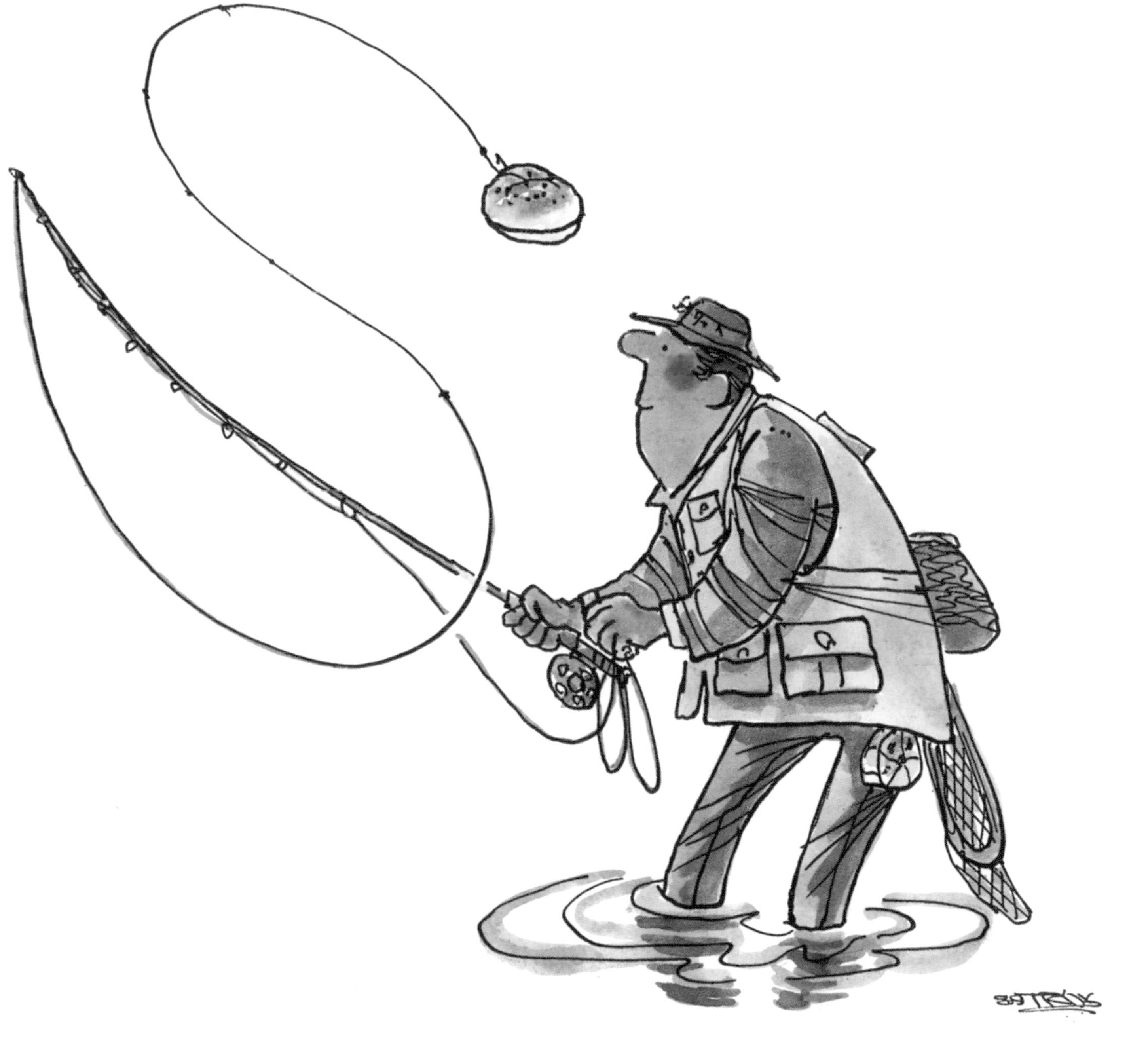

ROLL CAST

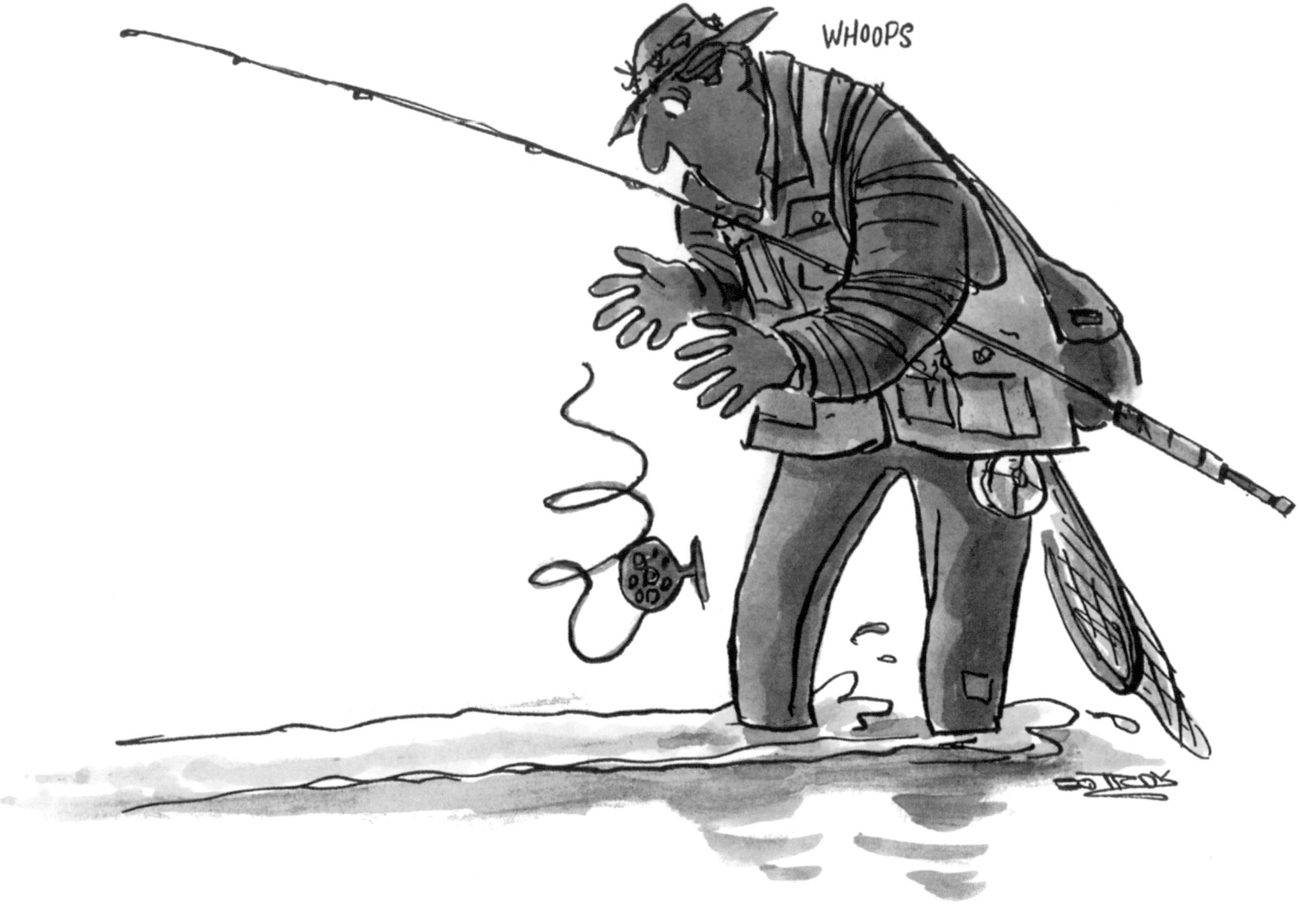
WHOOPS

DROP LINE

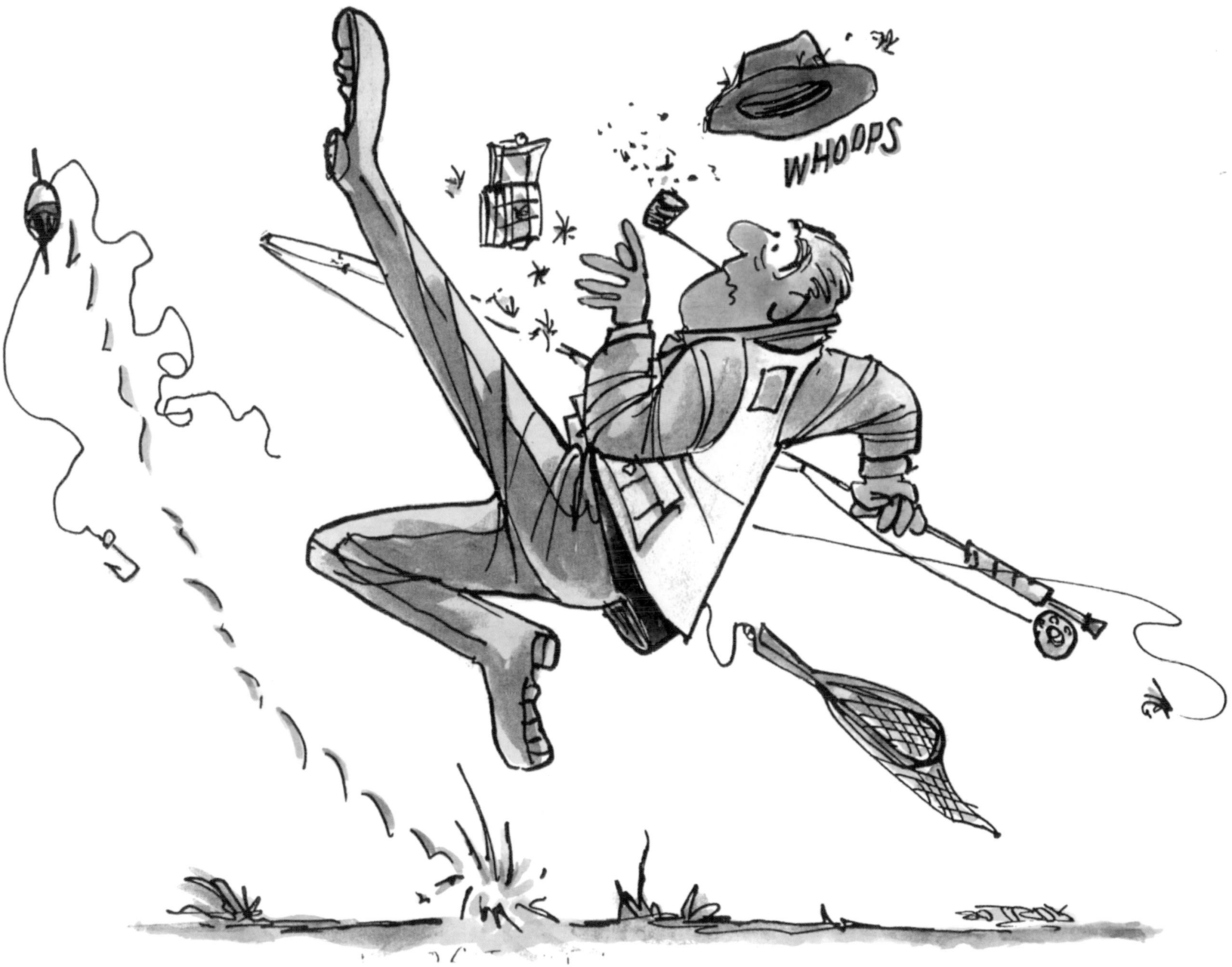
WHOOPS

FLOAT TRIP

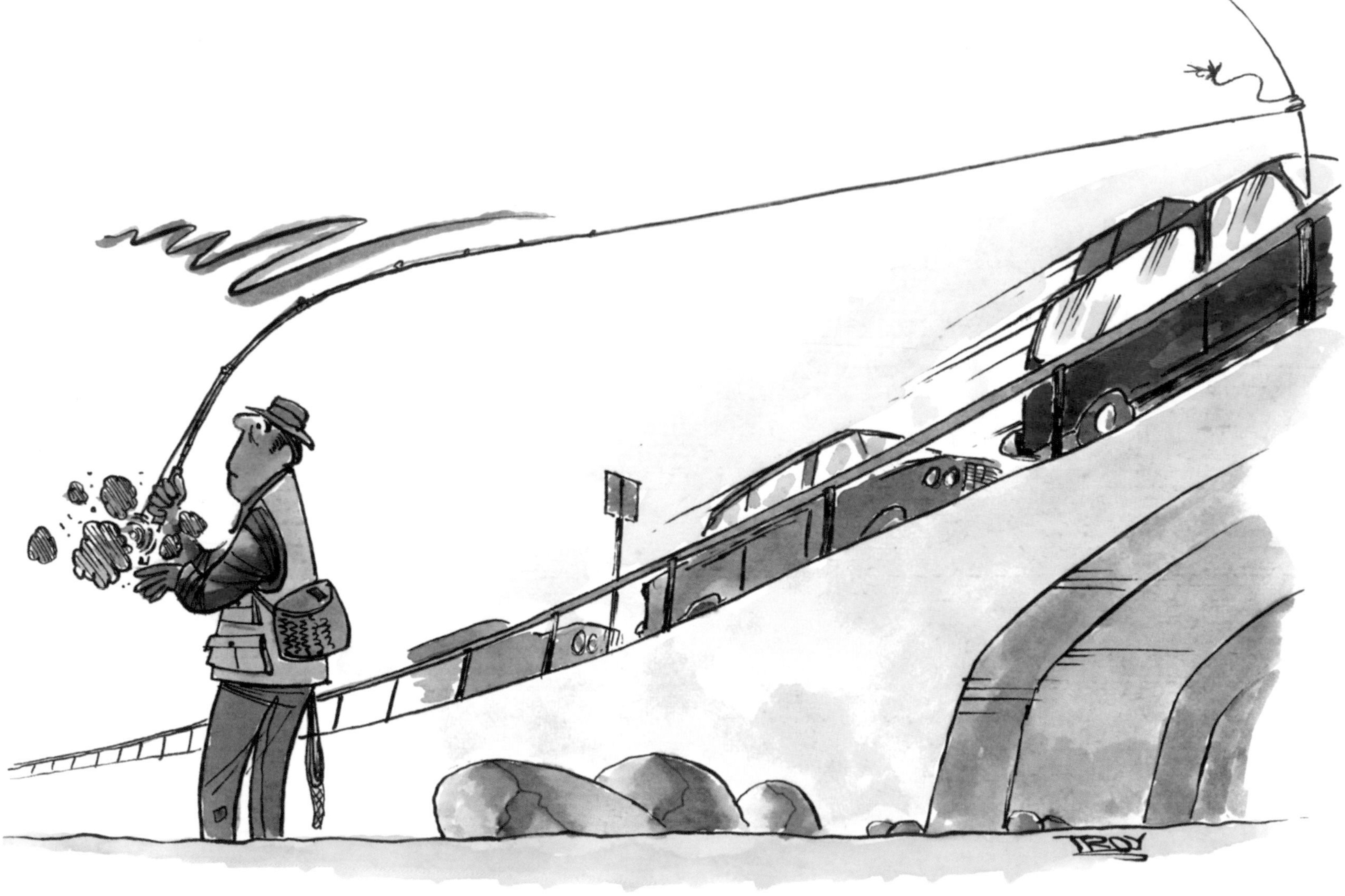

LONG FIRST RUN!

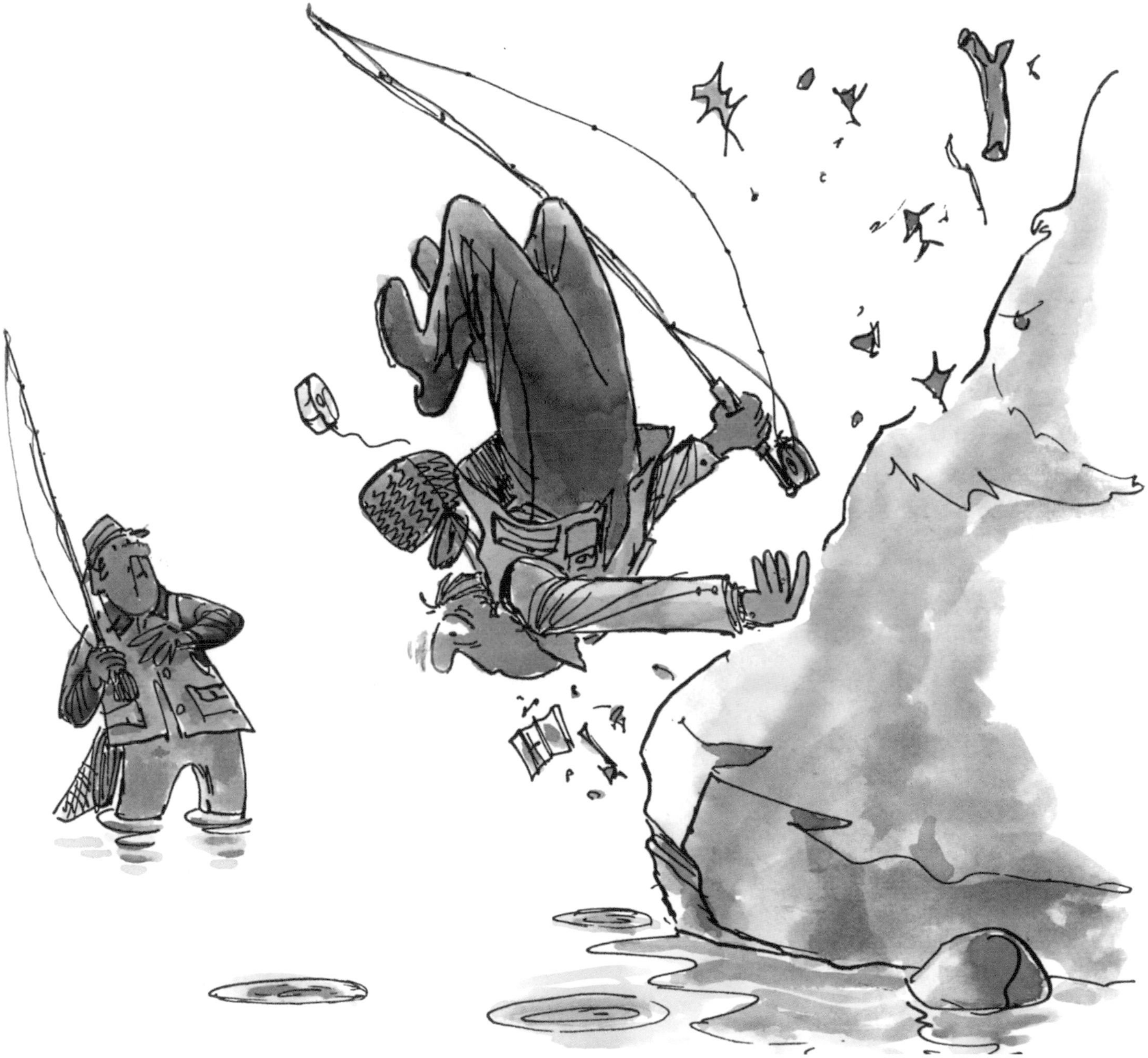

FALL FISHING

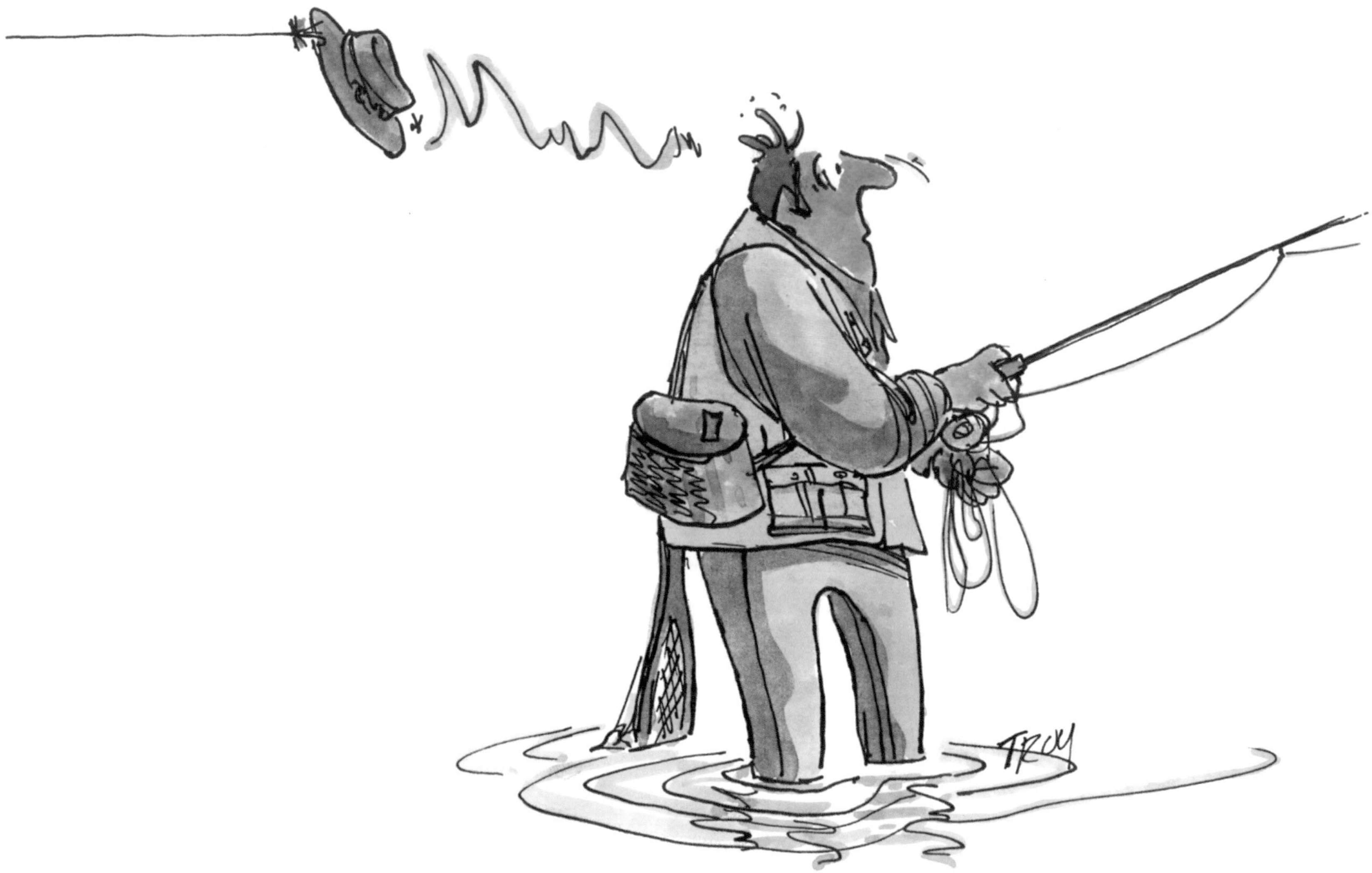
TROY

HAT TRICK

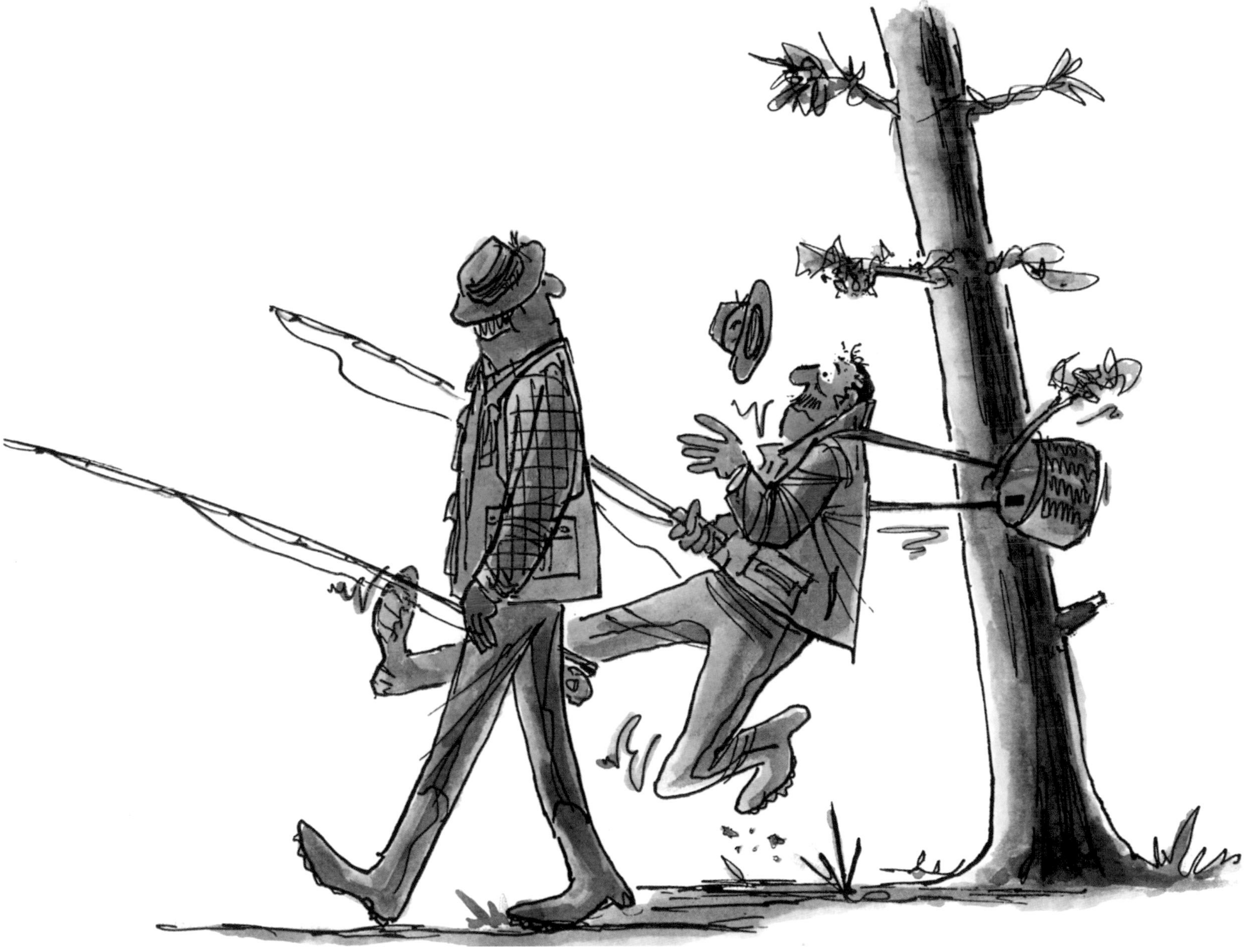

TREED!

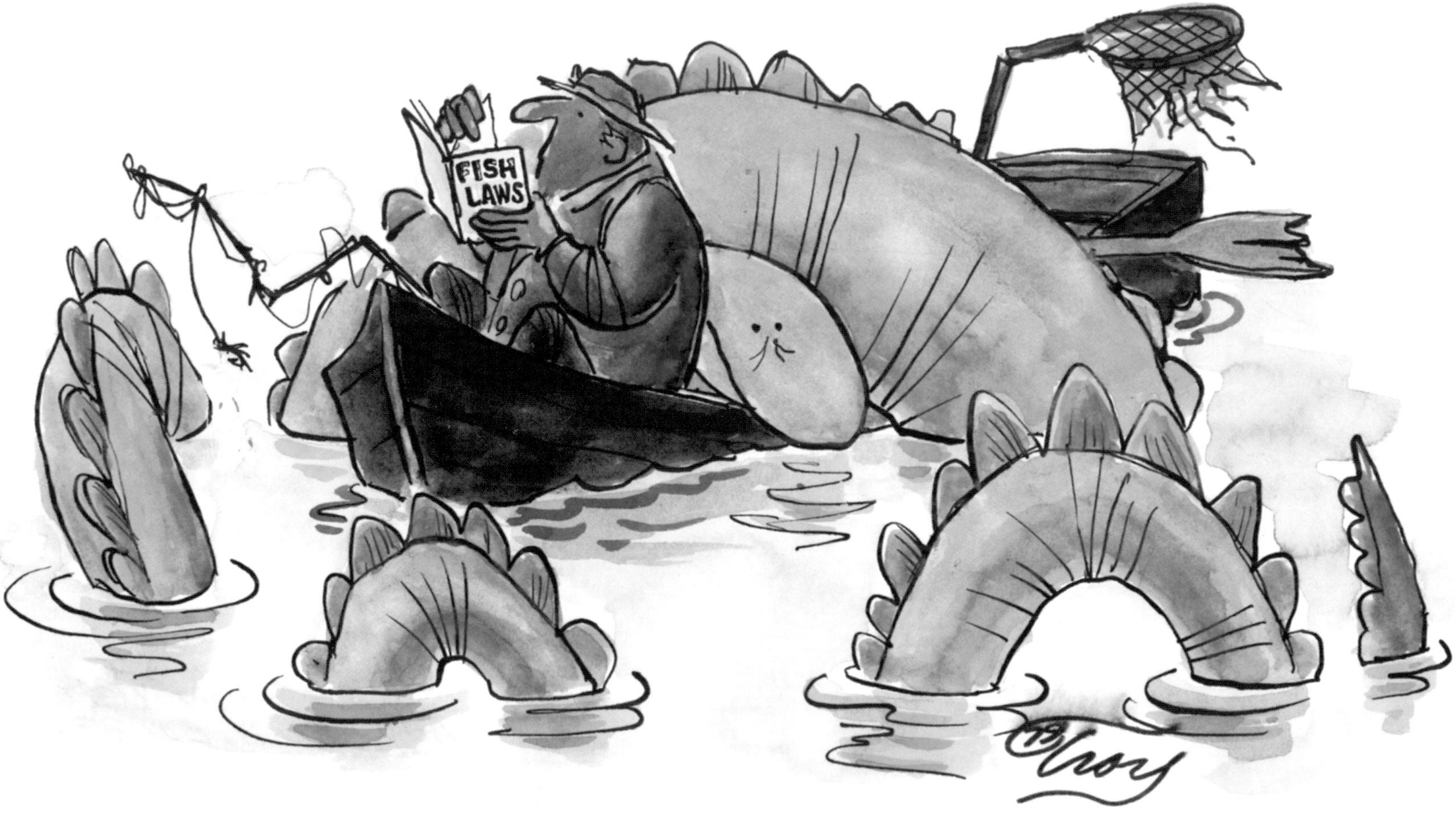
FISH LAWS

"I've been admiring your casting, but your choice of flies leaves a lot to be desired."

"I see you're a firm believer in the 'Large Bait, Large Fish Theory'."

"After buying the fly rod of my dreams I couldn't afford anything else."

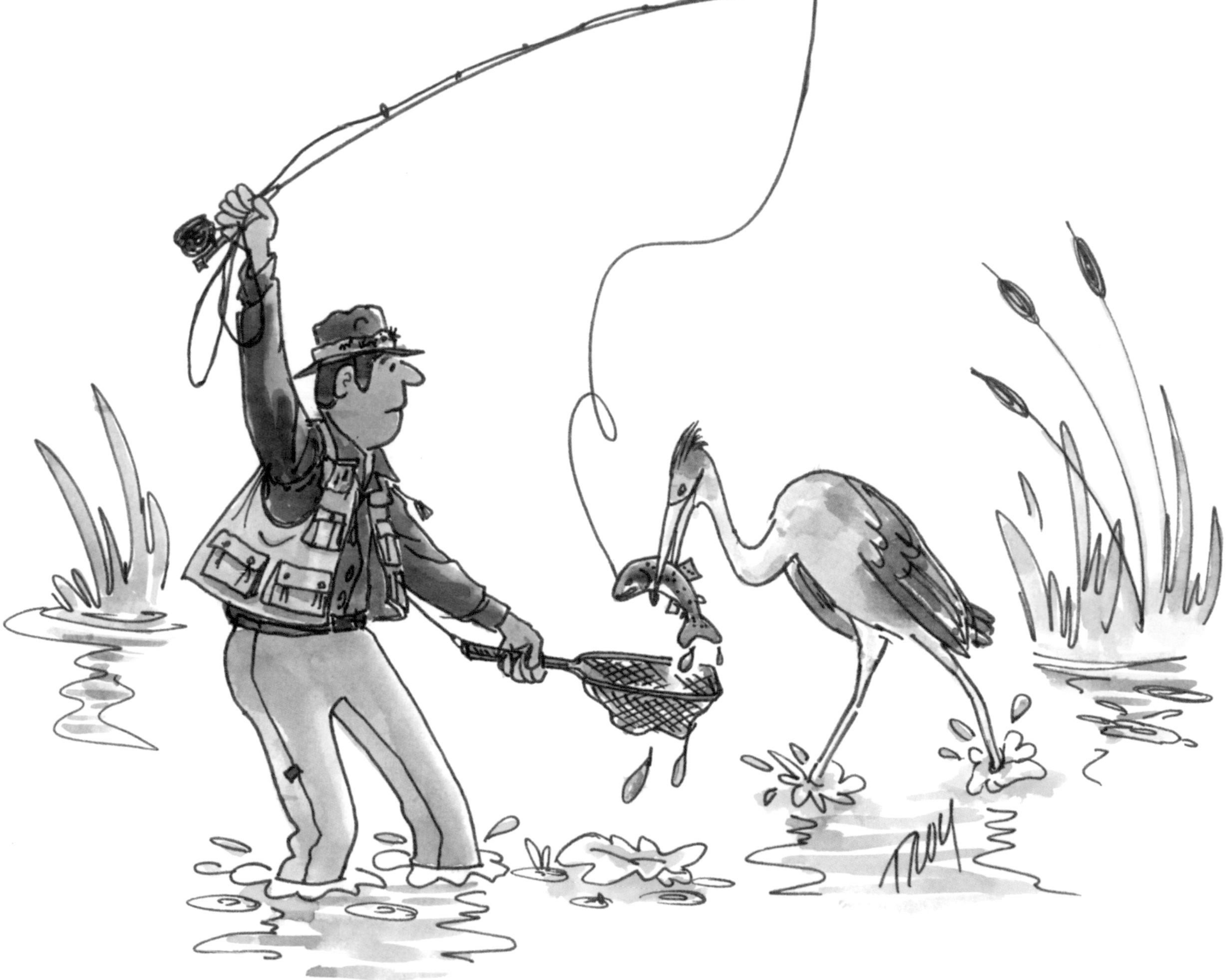
TROY

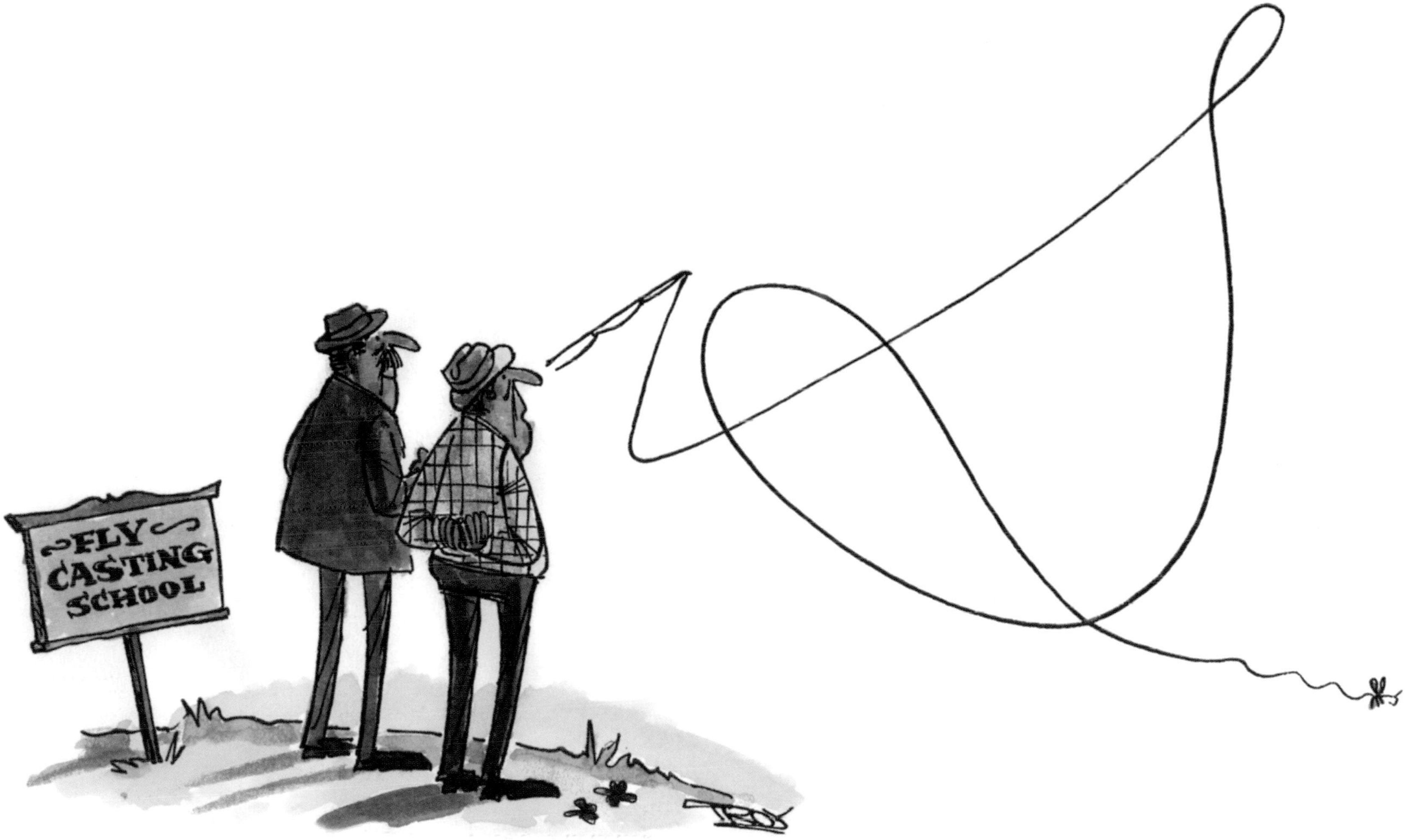
FLY
CASTING
SCHOOL

"As nice an 'S' cast as I've ever seen, Mr. Finlay, but I was thinking more in terms of a capital 'S', and not necessarily in script."

"By George, you're right again. Line speed is the main factor in making long casts!
But say, weren't you a brown trout the last time we talked?"

"What's he doing that we're not doing?"

"I'm sorry, I don't question the fairness of laws. I just enforce them."

"So, I'm the first salmon you ever hooked on a fly, eh?"

"No, Elsworth. Our catch and release program applies only to fish—not violators."

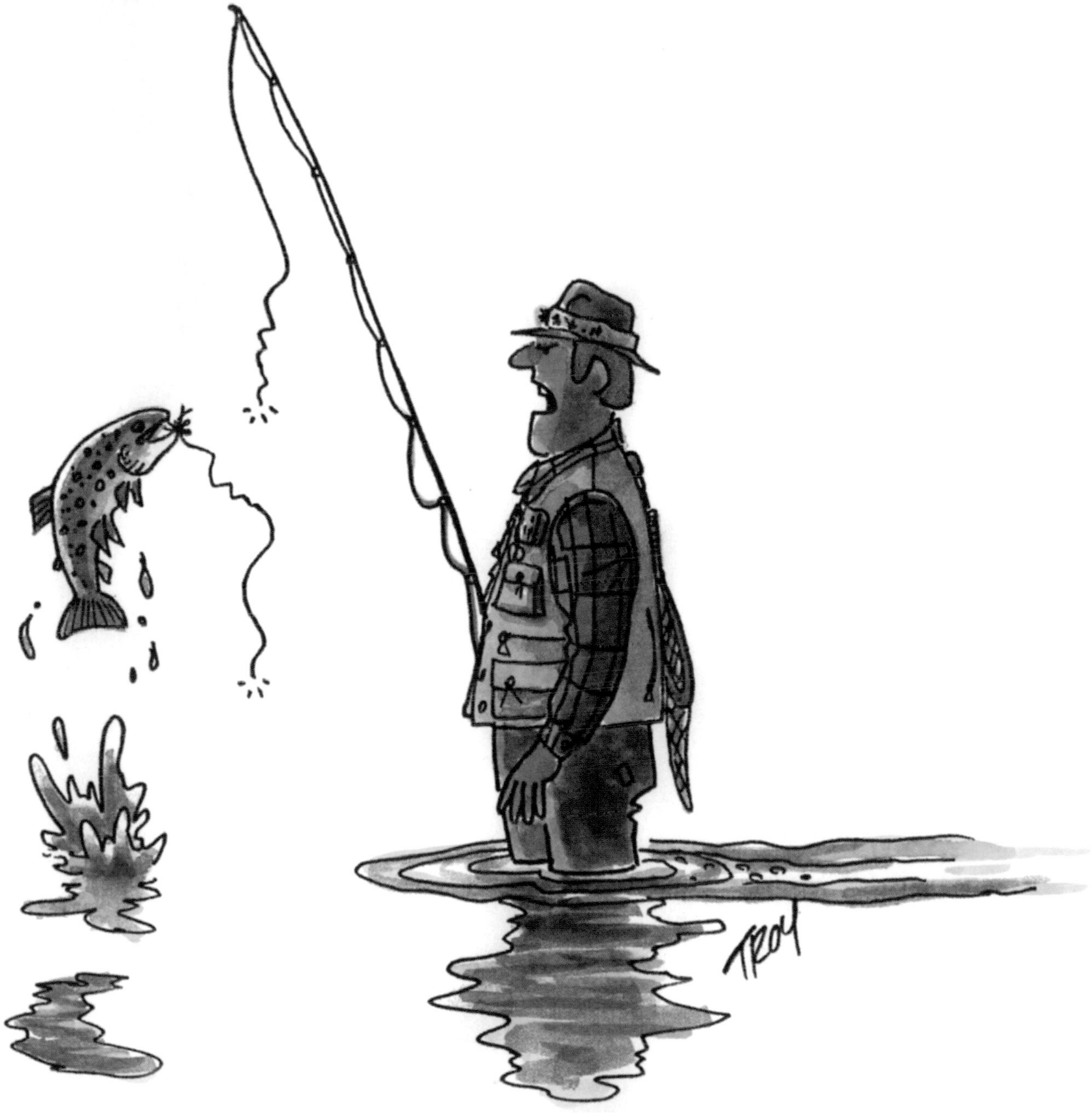
TROY

"I see it! I SEE IT!"

"Relax, Ed, you're too tense."

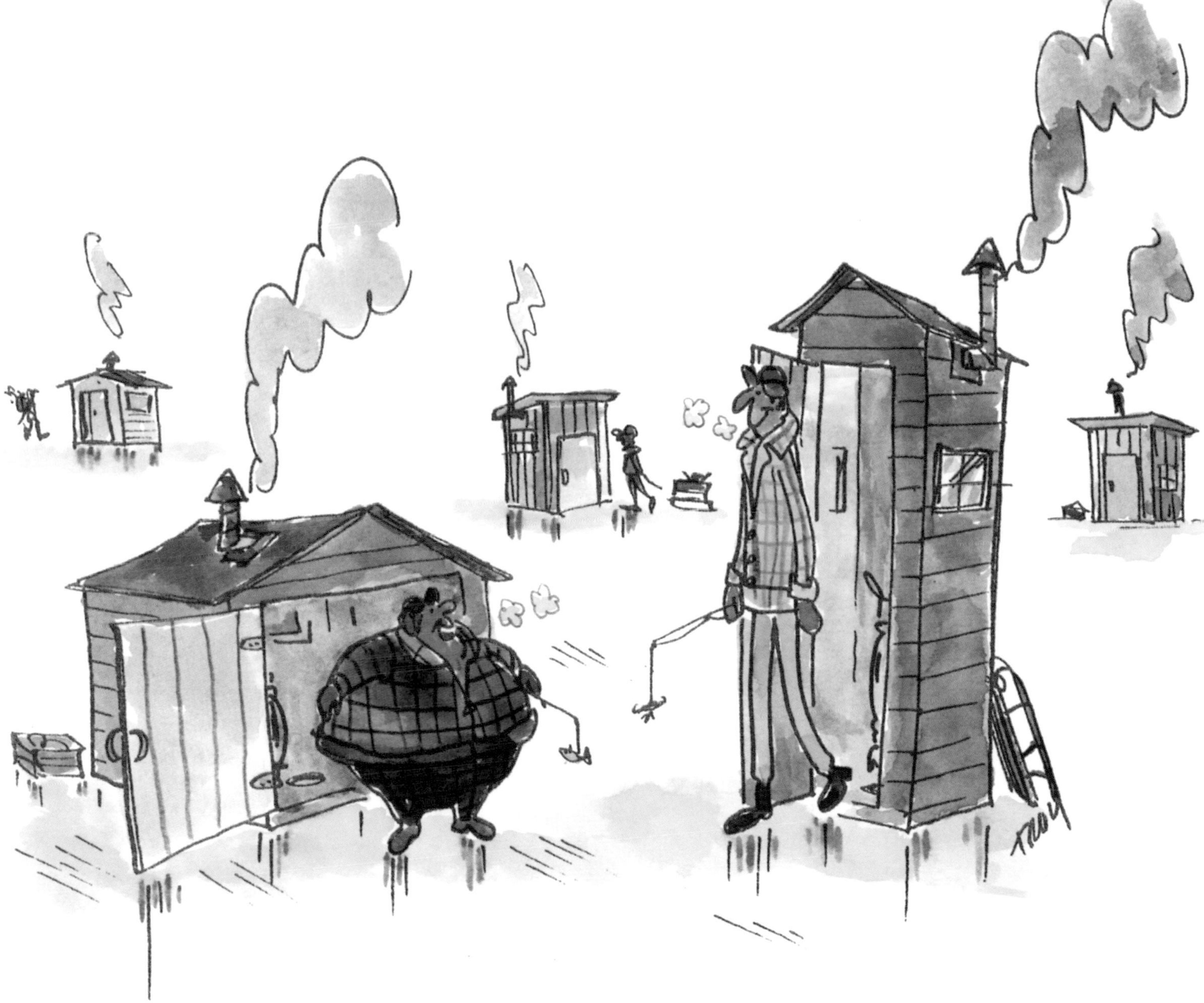

"How they biting?"

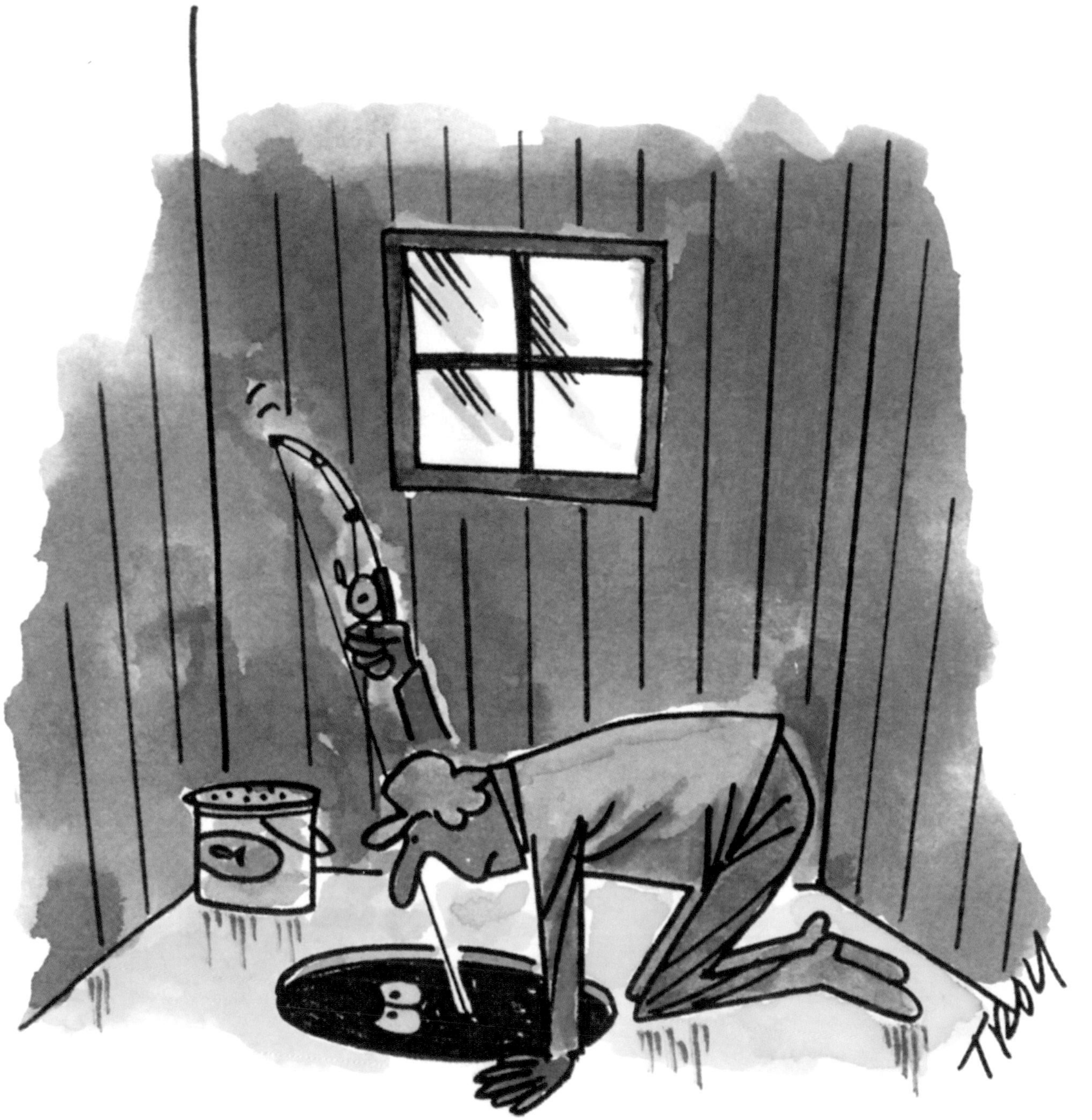

"Is that the way you get your kicks, by watching us spawn?!"

"Rain drops keep fallin' on my head, but that doesn't mean . . ."

"I caught a muskie before Herb did. Since then life has been pure hell."

"I don't really care that you tie flies better than me, or that you can cast farther, or even that you catch more fish than I do. What gets me is that you look so damn good doing it!"

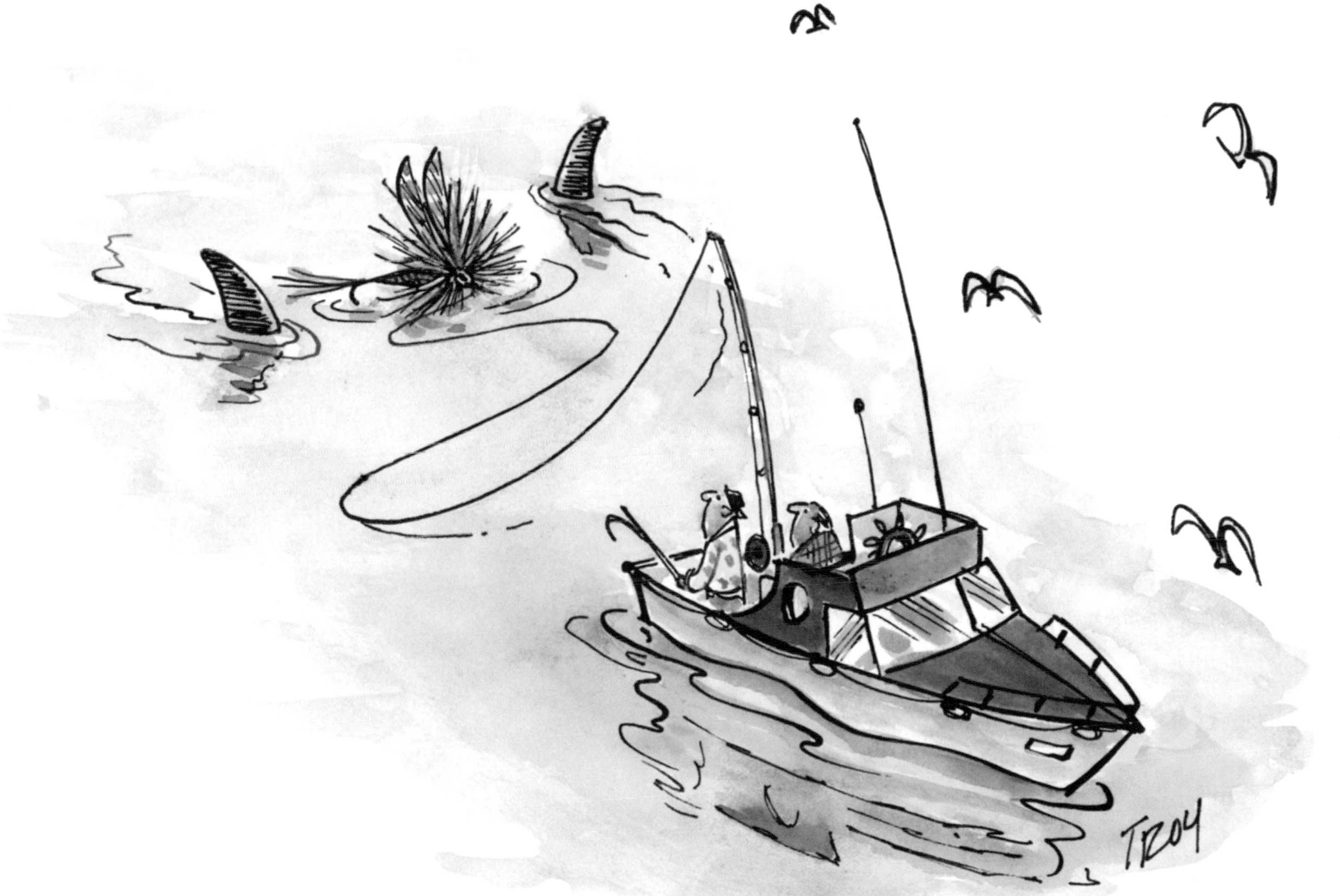
TROY

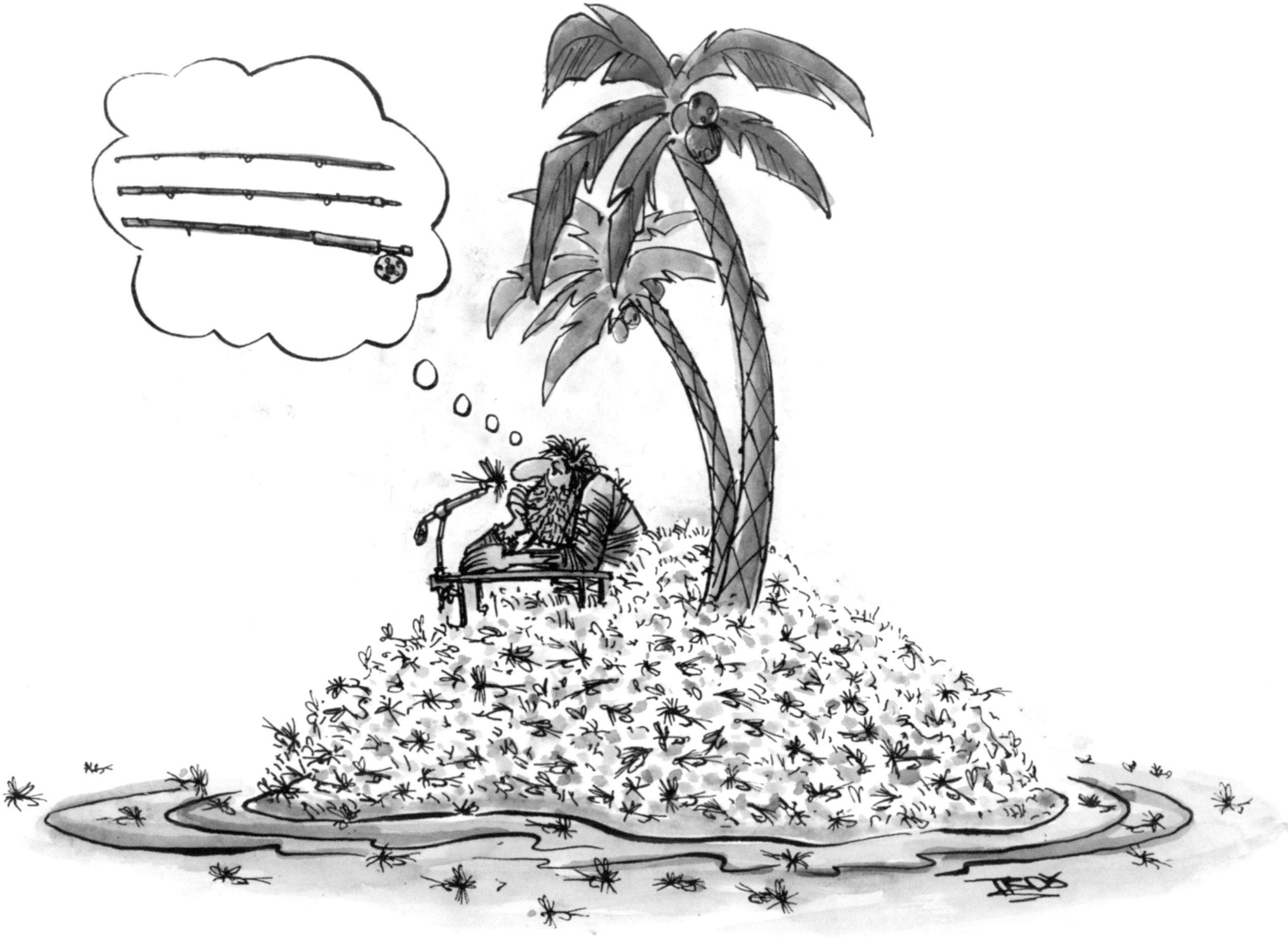

"Isn't the fly supposed to hit the water now and then?"

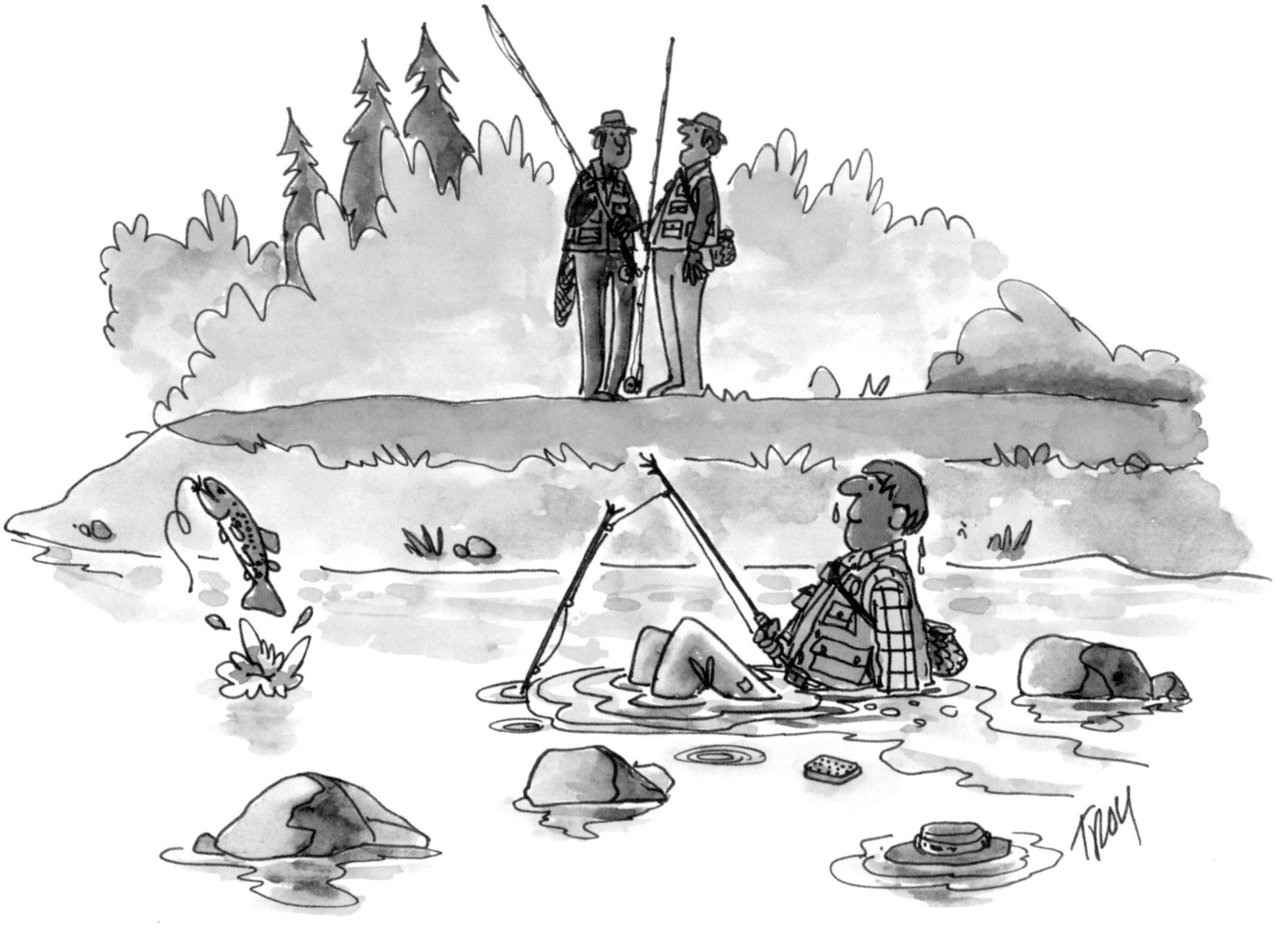
TROY

"Al's been into catch and release for years, but it's not been on a voluntary basis."

"Someday you're going to meet someone who's not going to take all that abuse!"

"Nothing like a storm front to get those fish moving!"

"Snagging. Snagging! Hey, do I look like the kind of guy that would be snagging?"

"Never mind me—which fly are they rising to?!"

"Whatever this Is, it's coming!"

"Wow, look at those Chinooks spawning! You'd think it was a matter of life and death!"

"You should have been here yesterday— they were really biting."

"We got two small bass and three large speeding tickets."

"I'm always chasing Rainboowwws. . . ."

"I'd like to think there's a *lunker* in every pool that I fish."

"Oh good, that saves us the trouble of coming to your house to see your muskie."

"When are you going to get caught up in this 'catch and release' thing?"

"Every chance I get, I'm outta that office."

"All you care about is trout fishing."

"Still determined to catch that lunker trout on a dry fly?"

"Hey listen, that's not what I meant by 'casting a fly'."

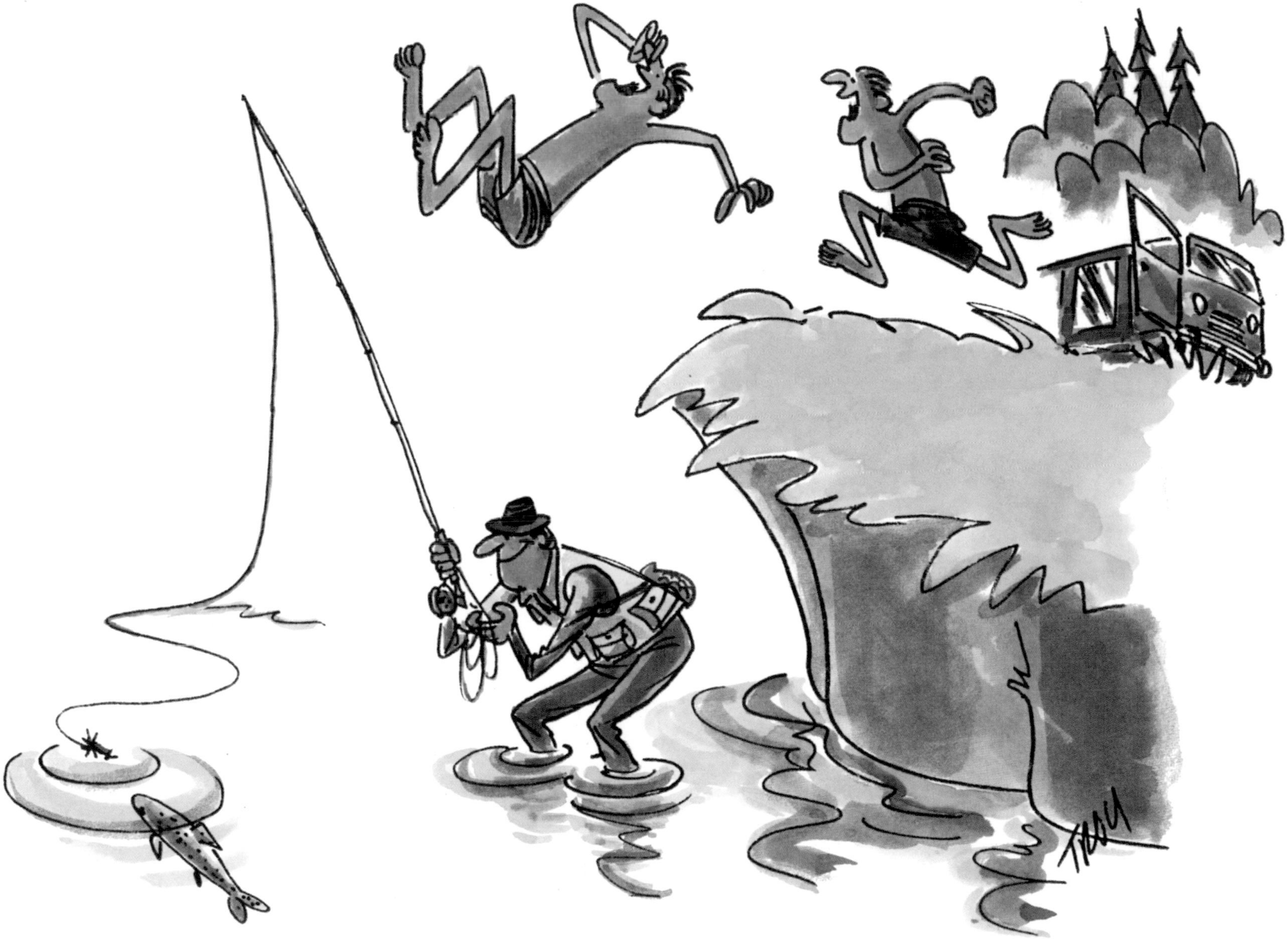

"I see you're into ice fishing."

"I caught them on a size twelve Dark Hendrickson dry fly. What are you using?"

"C'mon, lighten up and troll the right way."

"There, there, Mr. Fletcher, the world doesn't begin and end with a fanwing Royal Coachman."

This is a good idea as long as we don't run into a three hundred pound brown trout."

"I can tell you, it wasn't easy."

"Tom landed a muskie today. Without a net."

"They'll start to rise at noon. Take my word for it—*I know.*"

"Best cutthroat guide in the business."

"We'll look back on this someday and laugh."

"Ice fishing season is never quite long enough for Edgar."

"Really into ultra-light, aren't you."

"Wouldn't you know it—just when they were biting good!"

"I caught some flies so I can go fly-fishing with you."

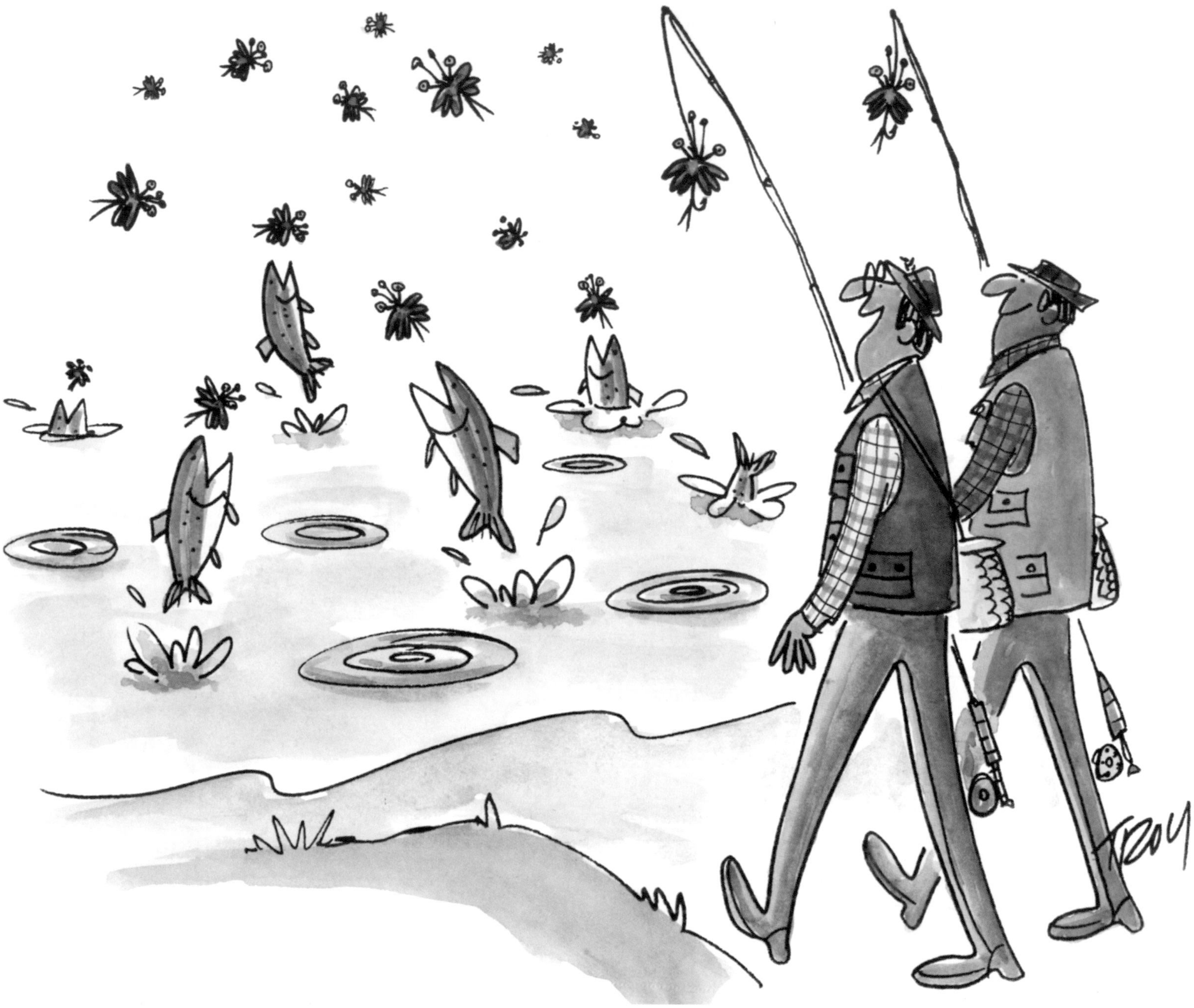
TROY

"Ah, what luck!"

"Walter, there's a *musica domestica* in my soup."

"It was her late husband's most prized possession and she wouldn't part with it. So I bought the old lady, too."

"Your fly snapped off three hours ago, young man, but you're casting so beautifully I didn't want to disturb you."

"No, your daddy is not going to the moon, he's going bass fishing."

"Have you ever thought of just using a nice sucker for muskie bait?"

"This is Mr. Edwards. He ties our midges."

"Does this stream have a slippery bottom?"

"Control yourself, man, it's only a few more days to Opening Day!"

"When does salmon season start?!"

"Every day I ask myself, 'Is it worth all that misery going out in the rottenest weather to catch a few lousy little fish?'. . . and before I can answer this idiot in me says, 'Yup'."

"Try by that old stump. There's usually a good one hiding there."

"Something tells me dry flies won't do the job today."

"We seldom eat fish. I don't like them, and George can't catch them."

"You haven't lived 'till you've fished a storm front!"

"Ah, there's a productive pattern."

"I don't think George really cares for the Islands."

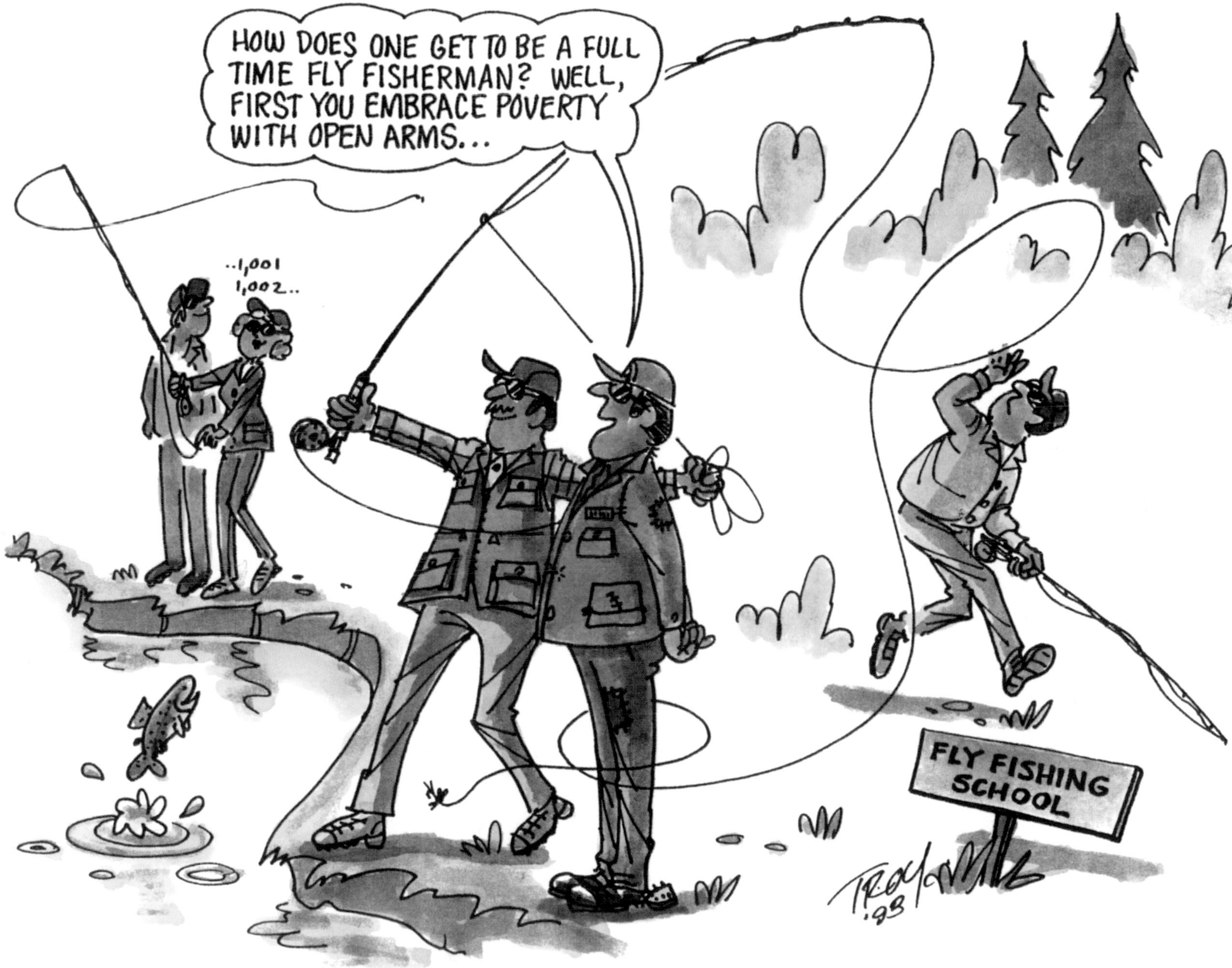
HOW DOES ONE GET TO BE A FULL TIME FLY FISHERMAN? WELL, FIRST YOU EMBRACE POVERTY WITH OPEN ARMS...
..1,001 1,002..
FLY FISHING SCHOOL
TROY '83

"*You* ask if they're biting."

"He's a politician, so don't even ask him how many fish he caught."

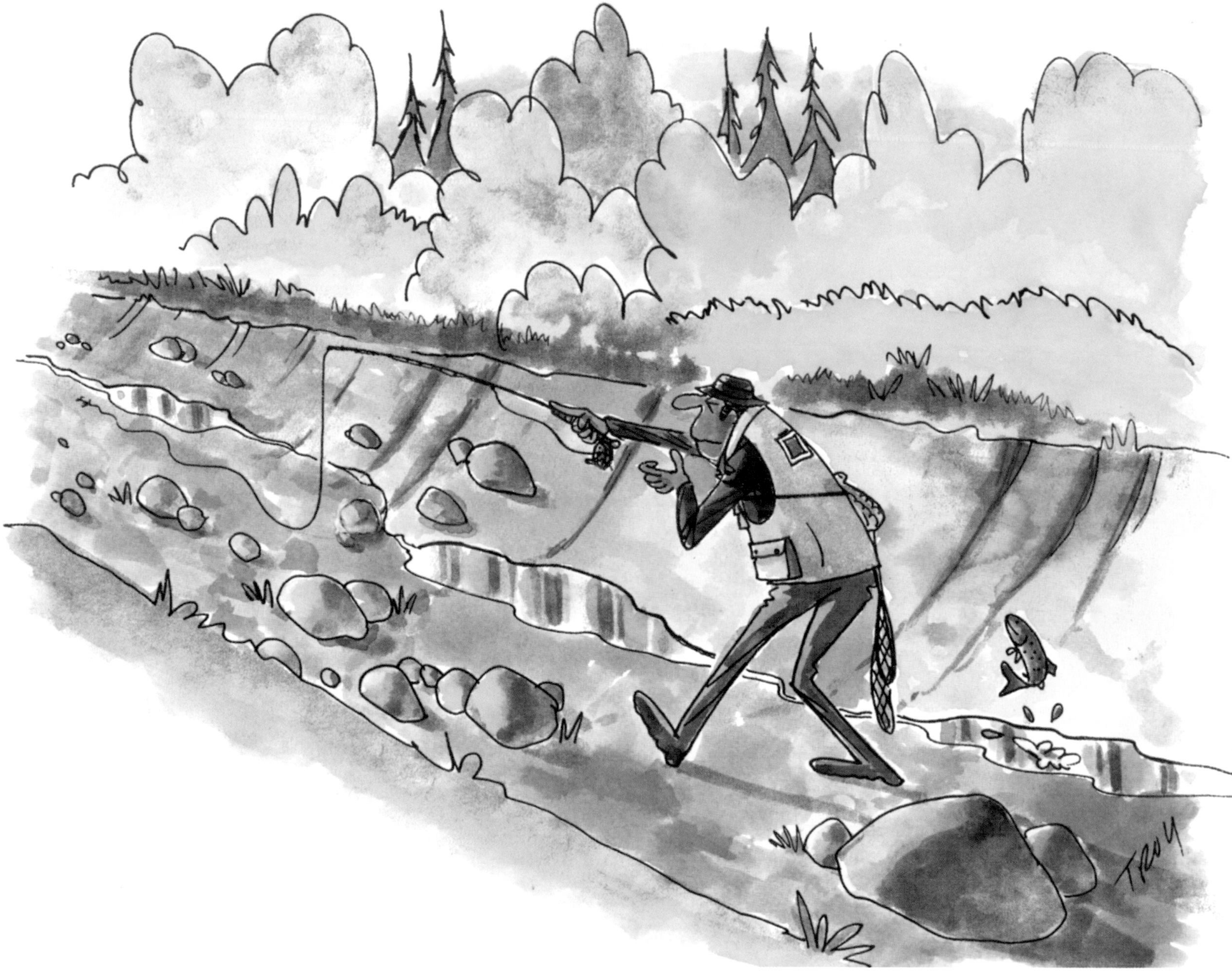
TROY

"You've changed, Al, ever since you started fly-fishing!"

"Wet flies, dry flies, they're all the same to me—help yourself."

"I'll be darned—there're my sinkers, my watch, my knife . . ."

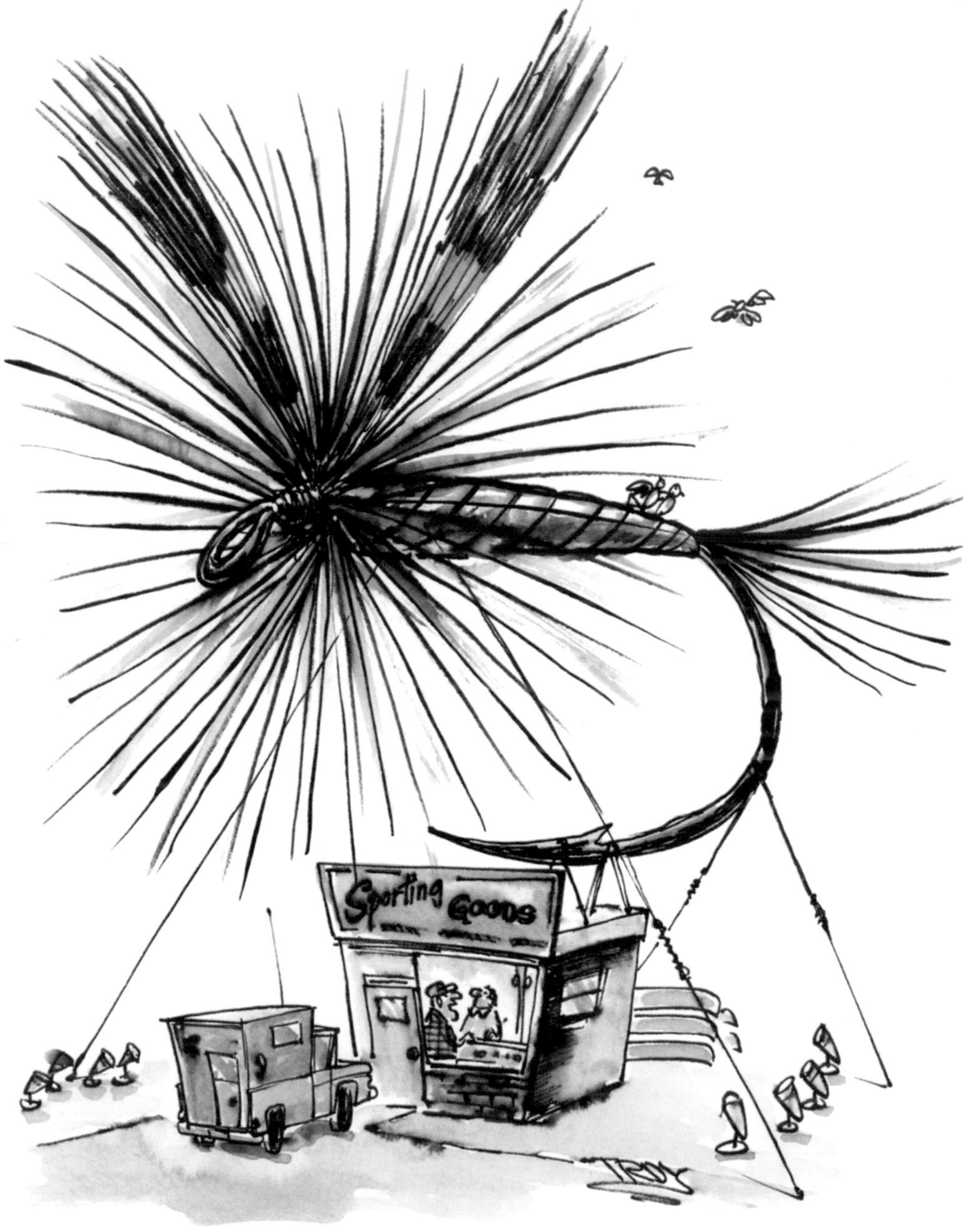
Sporting Goods

“Do you sell trout flies?”

"That part of the stream has a lot of rainbows in it."

"I remember when these were virgin waters."

"I don't like the looks of this fish, Bobby Joe."

"You sewed a zipper on my what, dear?"

"You didn't really *have* to."

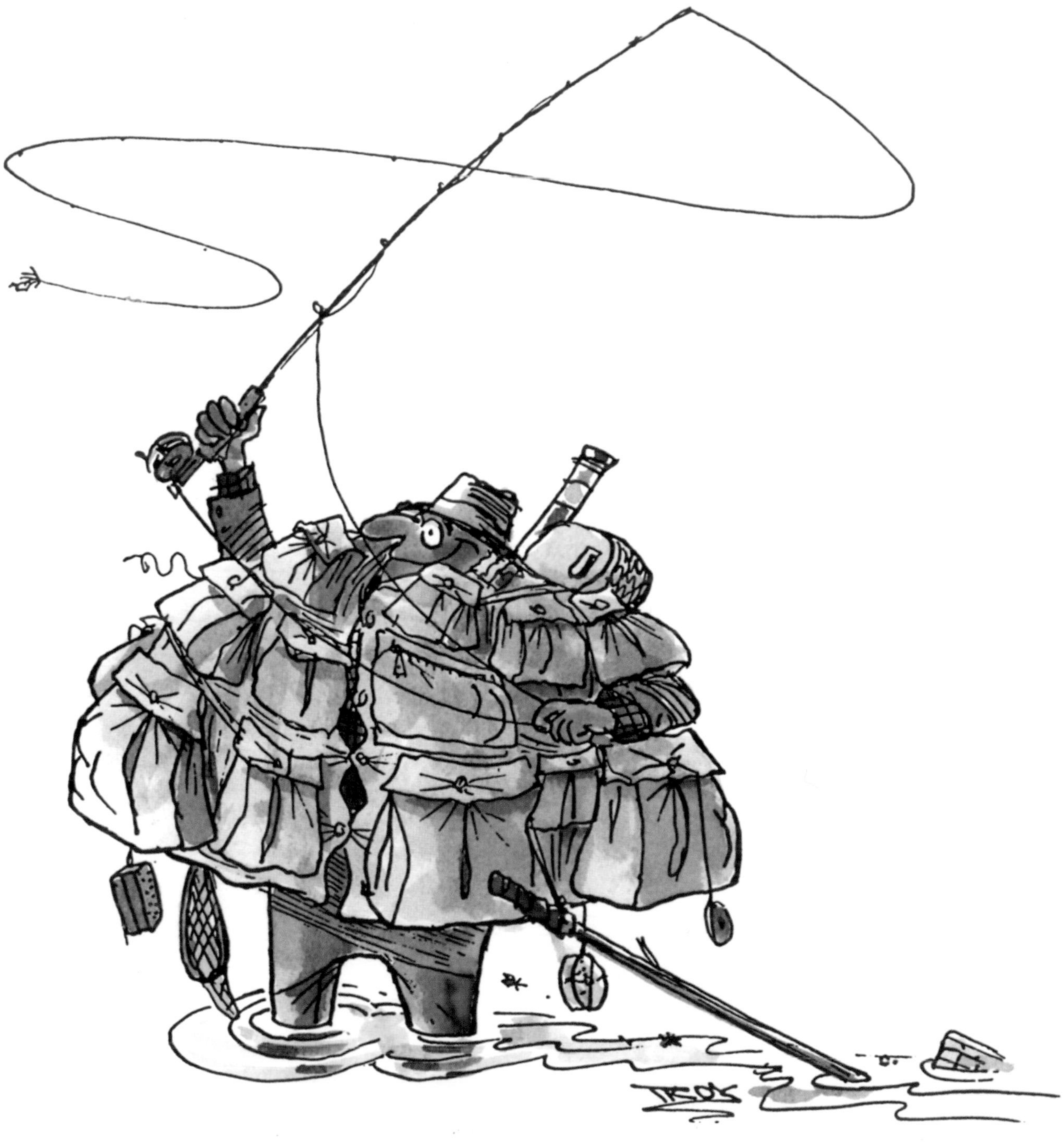

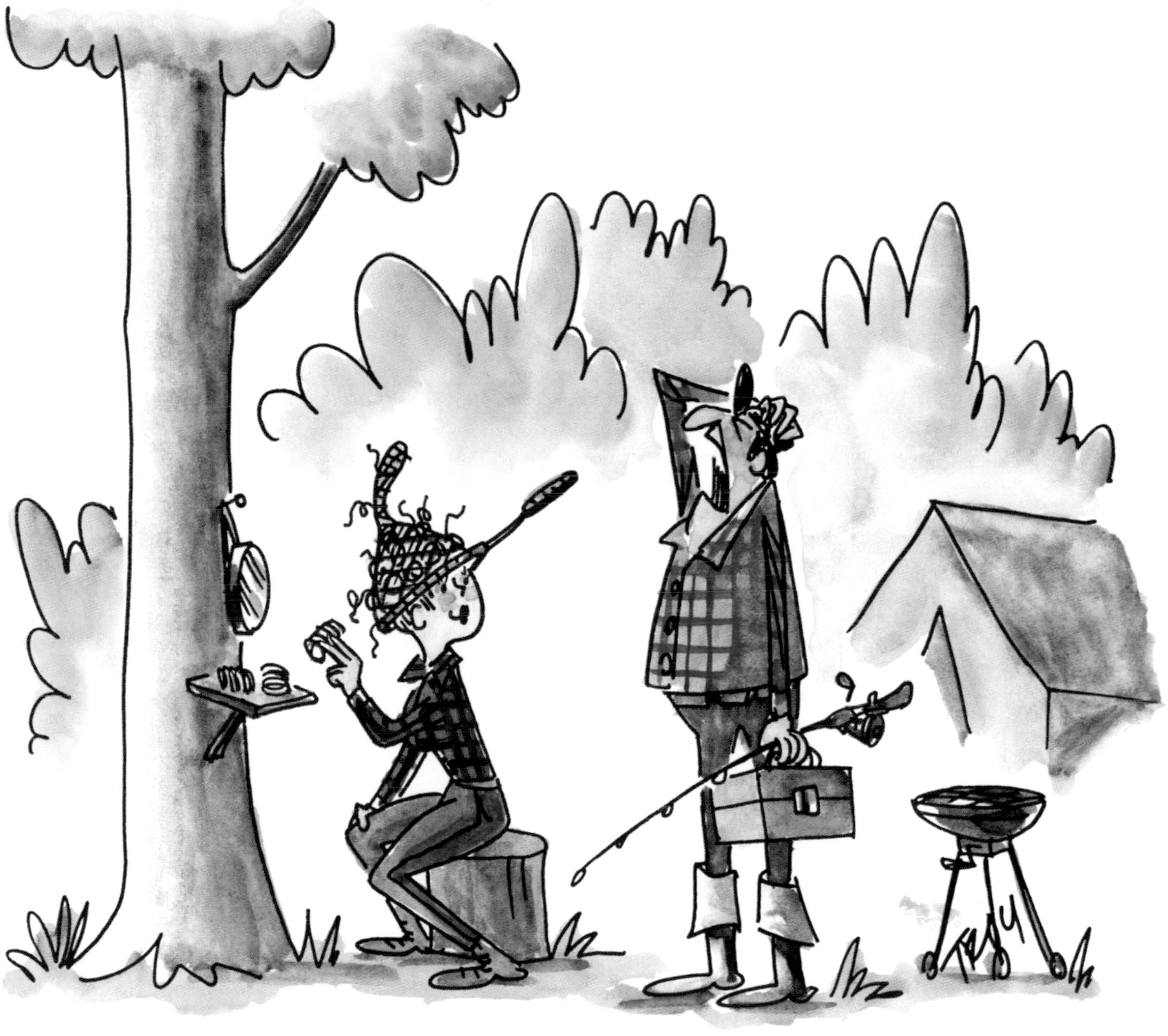

"My landing net!"

"Ed missed a nice trout in that hole last week. He takes everything personally."

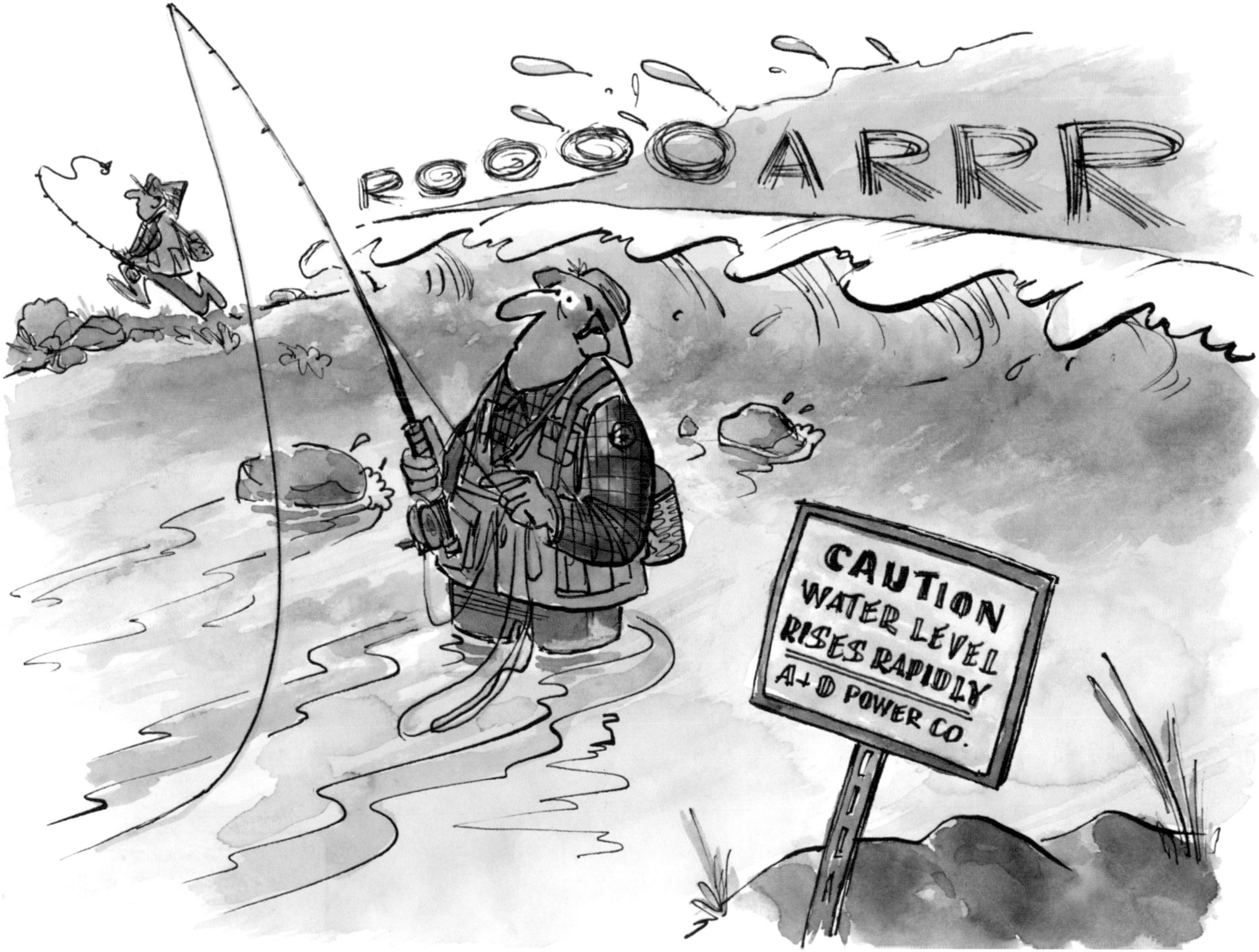
ROOOOOARRR
CAUTION
WATER LEVEL
RISES RAPIDLY
A+D POWER CO.

"So . . . how long have you fished for walleyes?"

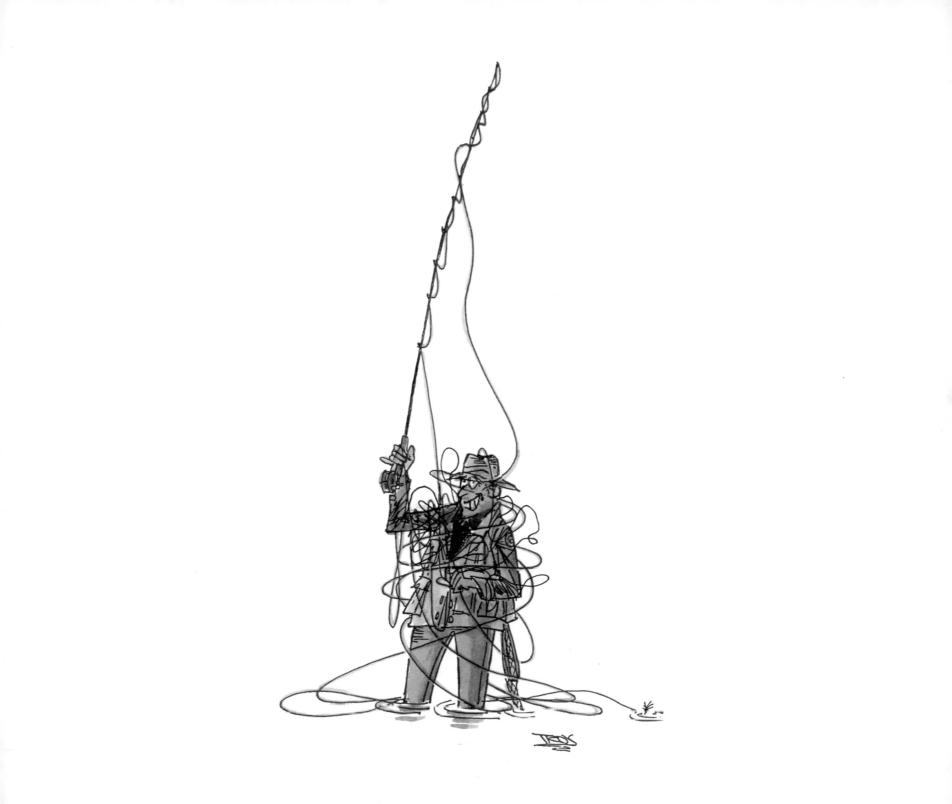

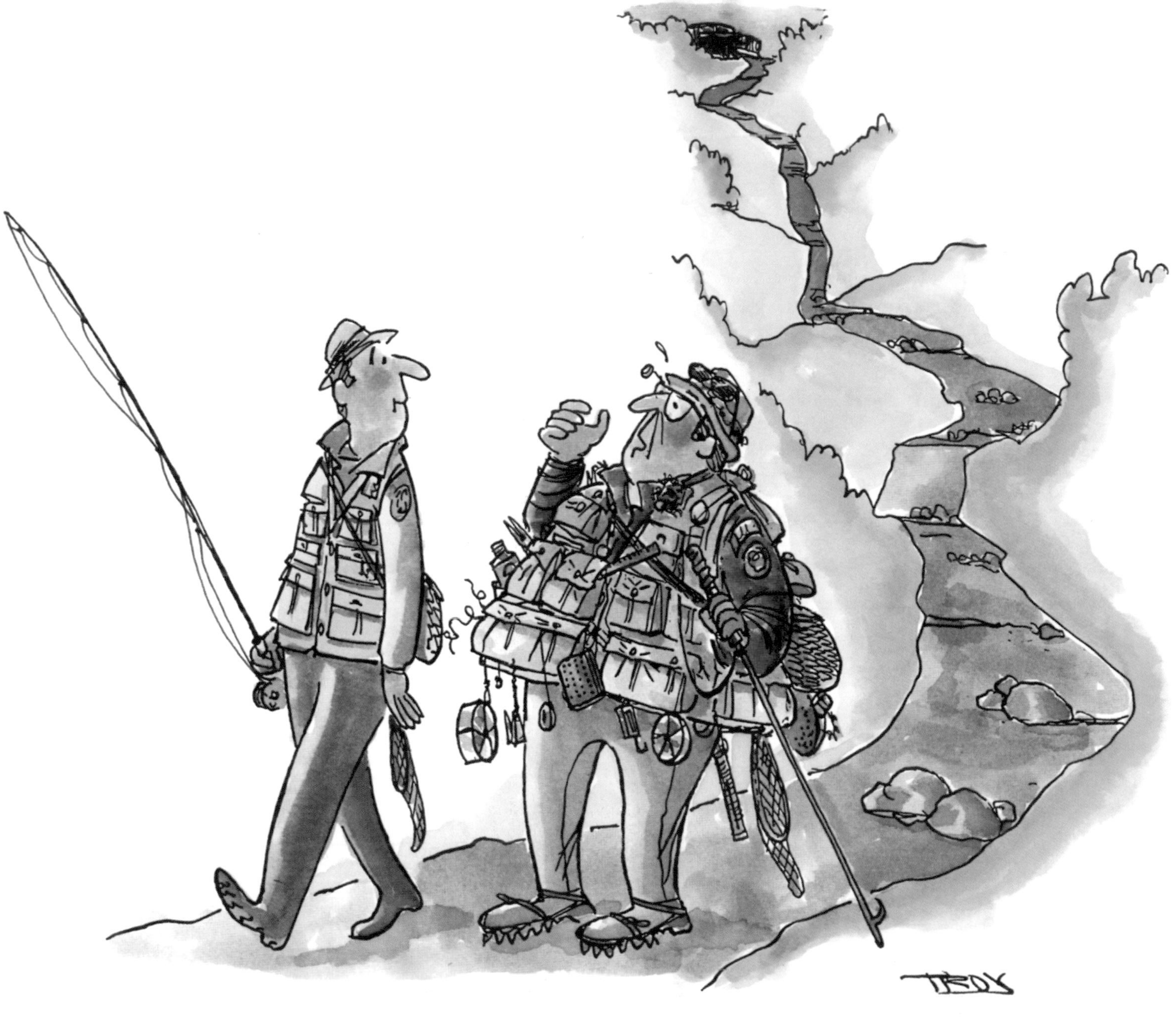

"I forgot my fly rod."

"Sonny, I've *forgotten* more than you'll ever know about fly-fishing."

"Get rid of everything red—your jacket, your bandanna, Red Ibises, Mickey Finns, Parmachene Belles, Royal Coachmans. . . ."

"I'll have a Ginger Quill, and make it extra dry, please."

"A bait fisherman, eh? And just how did you slip through?"

"I see you like doing things the old-fashioned way."

"She likes to go with me, but really doesn't care that much for fishing."

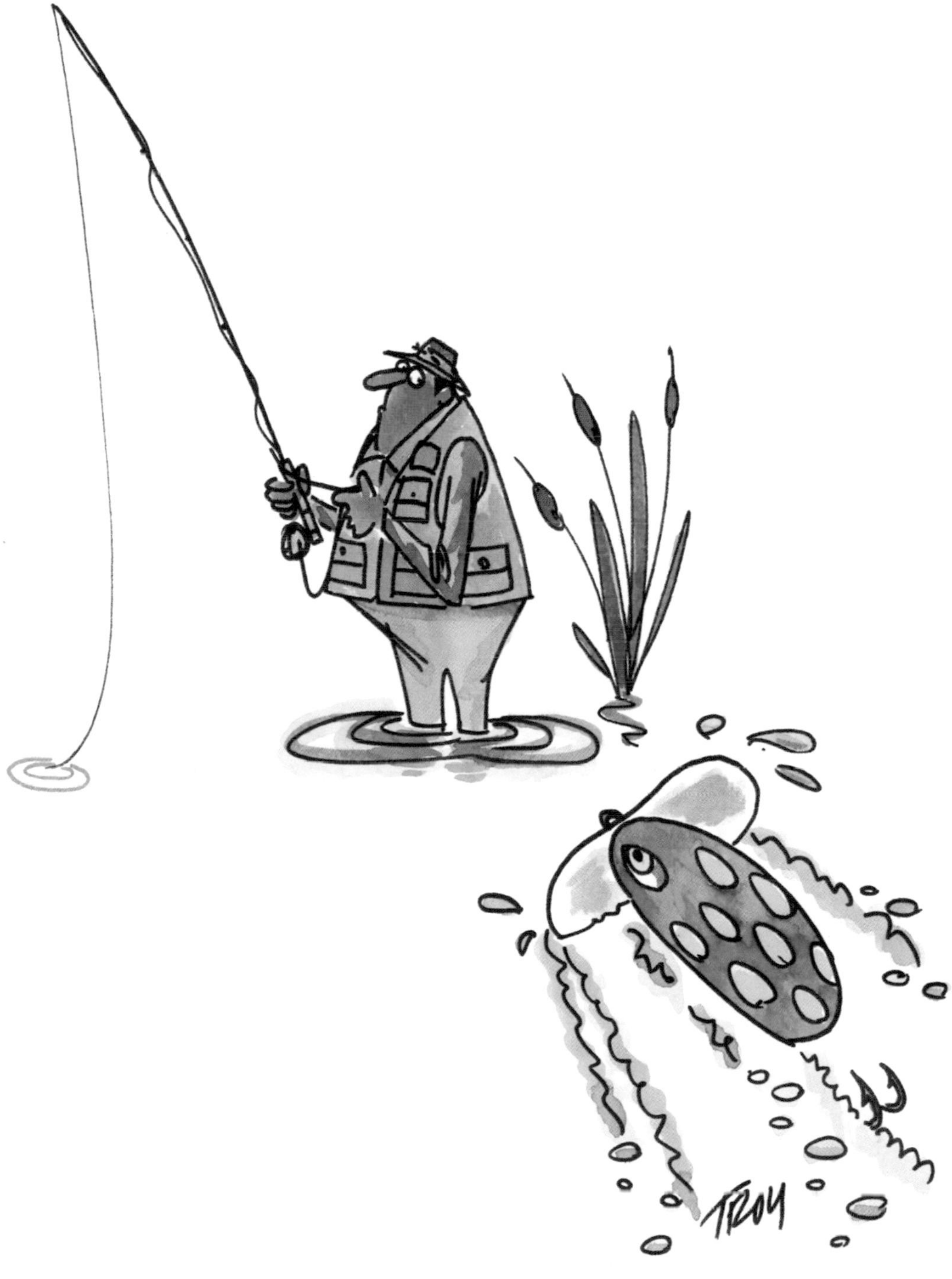
TROY

"Ben's been tying flies for about a year now—matter of fact, it's the same fly."

"Whoa, sorry, didn't see the sign!"

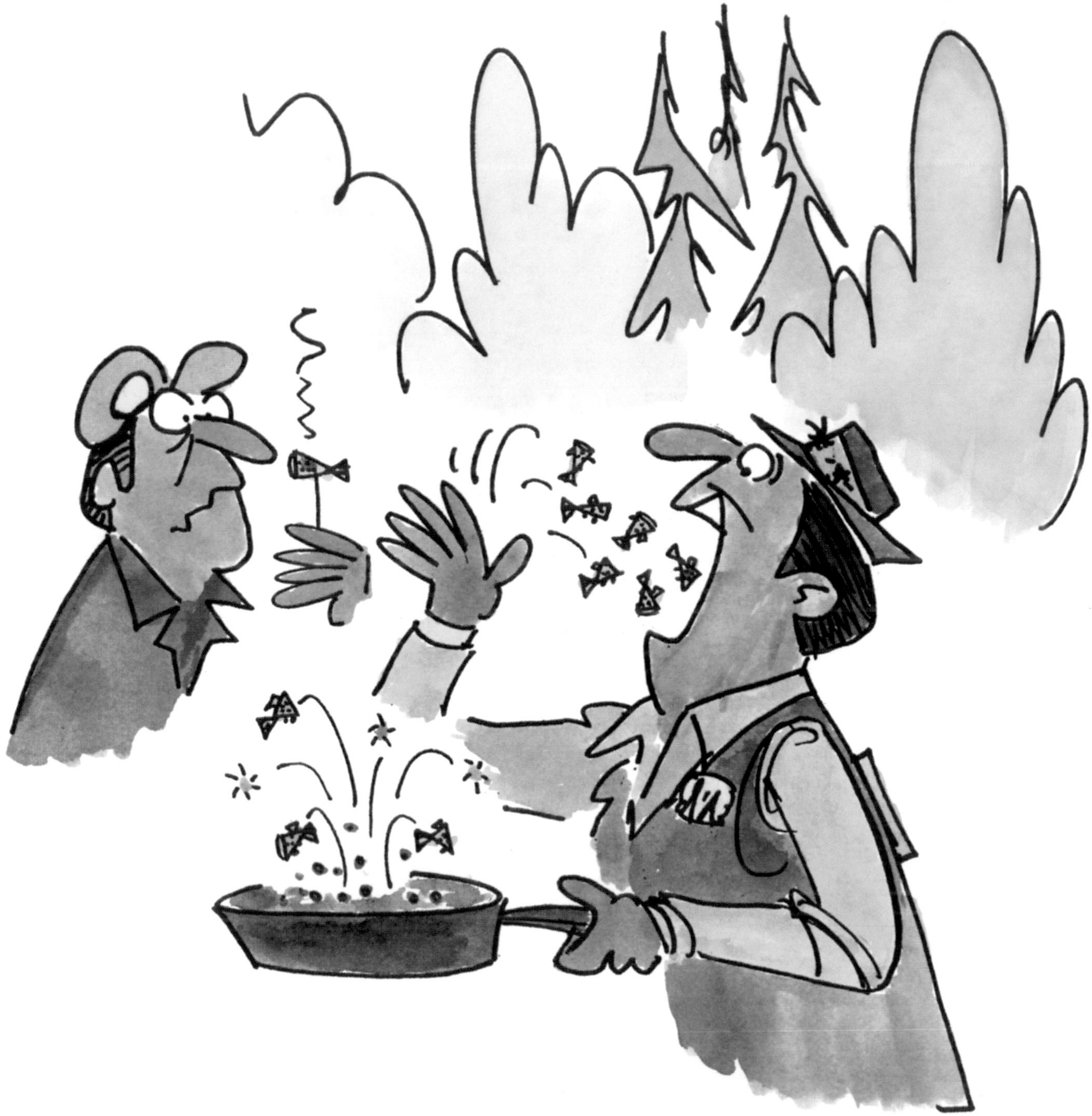

"Now let's see if I have this straight. You brought the muskie up to the boat and, being an old-time bass fisherman, you grabbed it by the lower jaw to immobilize it. . . ."

"Edwin lives for salmon fishing."

"You want a real fish taker? Garden hackle, that's what!"

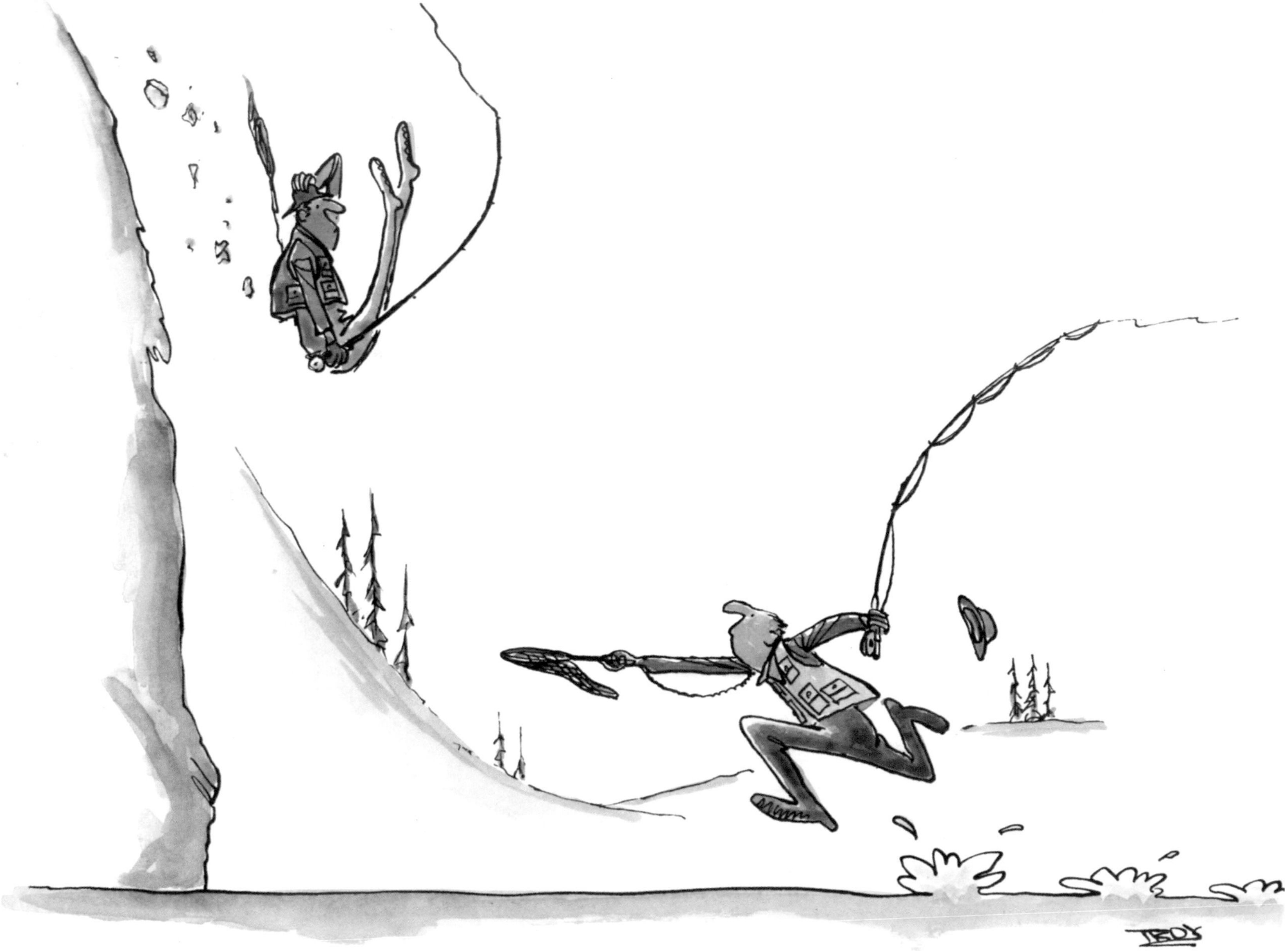